D0467079

Praise for
Identity: Your Passport to Success

"I wish someone like him [Stedman Graham] had been around to enlighten me at an age when finding myself and a career change or decision was within easy reach…all I needed, as he formulated, was a 'process.'"

—**Janice Jones**, Junior Achievement of Chicago

"Stedman Graham learned years ago that the secret to a successful life was to not let other people define him, but rather to define himself. As his thought-provoking book shows, finding your true identity is not as easy as it seems. Filled with inspiring real-life stories and life-changing insights, this page-turner of a book will snap you out of your complacency and make you think: Who are you, deep-down? What do you value, seriously? And what do you really want to do with your life? Don't miss this outstanding book."

—**Ken Blanchard**, coauthor of *The One Minute Manager®* and *Leading at a Higher Level*

"Get clear on who you are and live according to your own definition of success. Stedman Graham's *Identity* offers thought-provoking questions, strategies, and stories to expedite your journey to success. This is a must-read!"

—**Stuart Johnson**, Founder & CEO, Video*Plus* and *SUCCESS* Partners

"Stedman Graham is a man who stands tall and speaks from the heart. His insights and advice have provided a road map for success, which I have found invaluable."

—**Chas Edelstein**, Co-CEO, Apollo Group, Inc. (owner of University of Phoenix)

"*Identity* is an inspirational, honest, and clearly written book about how you can understand and make choices in your life where you matter and fit in a world full of personal challenges. It is a book of illuminating stories—Stedman's practical wisdom and process for personal success to get you to make your own way. This is a book everyone can use."

—**Elliott Washor**, Cofounder, Codirector, Big Picture Learning

"Stedman's book is once again delightful and insightful. The personal stories that are shared are so impactful. This kind of book takes us by the hand and brings to light the importance of knowing who we are and how our identity influences our lives and those around us. An insightful, inspirational, and much-needed book."

—**Laura Stansberry**, Senior VP, Wells Fargo Wealth Management Group

"In *Identity*, Stedman Graham skillfully walks you through a journey of self-discovery, at the end of which your purpose, path, and genius will be brilliantly obvious to you. In fact, this book could change your life. Descartes said: 'Know thyself.' I believe the best investment you can make is in growing and evolving your inner world; your outer world then becomes a perfect reflection of that evolved inner world. If you're ready to step up into a whole new level of your life's genius, *Identity* is an absolute must-read. Stedman's writing style is captivating; the personal stories and thoughtful questions and exercises in each chapter make this a book you'll go back to time and again!"

—**Mari Smith**, social media thought leader, author of *The New Relationship Marketing*

"It is often assumed, by ourselves and others, that we will just know what to do in life and how to do it, and that we have a clear picture of who we are. In *Identity*, Stedman Graham gives us a well-defined process for discovering the most important thing to know and understand about ourselves—our authentic identity. Even if we think we know a lot about ourselves, this book has the power to bring our knowledge to a level that will significantly shift our lives. Stedman includes engaging stories and thought-provoking questions that bring clarity and understanding to his transformational process."

—**Bobbi DePorter**, President, Quantum Learning Network / SuperCamp; author of *Quantum Success*, *Quantum Teaching*, and *8 Keys of Excellence*

"Stedman put into words what we have long held true at Gulfstream: There is no such thing as the status quo. To be successful, you need to have a vision and a road map to get you there. This book can serve as a blueprint for anyone looking to gain control of their life, both personally and professionally."

—**Larry Flynn**, President, Gulfstream Aerospace Corporation

"Most people acquiesce to mediocrity—not for the lack of God-given potential, but primarily because they value the camaraderie of the average beyond the uniqueness of excellence! Stedman Graham's *Identity* breaks rank and liberates us to set sail beyond our borders. All aboard!"

—**Bishop T.D. Jakes**, Senior Pastor, The Potter's House of Dallas, Inc.

"Stedman has nailed it! Your potential as a human being is based not on how the world defines you, but on how you define yourself. If you want your life to lead to true success, you first must find your true identity. This book will do exactly that. It will provide you with the tools, steps, and vision you need to impact your life and the lives around you. It's never too late to discover who you are!"

—**Randy Garn**, Chief Relations Officer, Prosper

"Stedman Graham shows us the importance of self identity and how living an authentic life gives you freedom. His process will guide you every step of the way."

—**Judge Greg Mathis**

"Stedman Graham teaches that you can transform your life through having a clear and defined understanding of who you are. When your identity is crystallized, so is your vision for the life you choose to lead, and that vision becomes your future. *Identity* is truly your passport to success—and significance! Thank you, Stedman, for being such a profound pathfinder."

—**Kevin Hall**, bestselling author of *Aspire* (the highest reader-rated book in personal development in 30 years)

Identity

Graham, Stedman.
Identity : your
passport to success /
c2012.
33305225644057
sa 05/24/12

Identity

Your Passport to Success

Stedman Graham

with

Stewart Emery and Russ Hall

Vice President, Publisher: Tim Moore
Associate Publisher and Director of Marketing: Amy Neidlinger
Editorial Assistant: Pamela Boland
Development Editor: Russ Hall
Operations Specialist: Jodi Kemper
Senior Marketing Manager: Julie Phifer
Assistant Marketing Manager: Megan Graue
Cover Designer: Chuti Prasertsith
Managing Editor: Kristy Hart
Senior Project Editor: Lori Lyons
Copy Editor: Krista Hansing Editorial Services
Proofreaders: Apostrophe Editing Services, Gill Editorial Services
Senior Compositor: Gloria Schurick
Manufacturing Buyer: Dan Uhrig

© 2012 by Stedman Graham
Pearson Education, Inc.
Publishing as FT Press
Upper Saddle River, New Jersey 07458

FT Press offers excellent discounts on this book when ordered in quantity for bulk purchases or special sales. For more information, please contact U.S. Corporate and Government Sales, 1-800-382-3419, corpsales@pearsontechgroup.com. For sales outside the U.S., please contact International Sales at international@pearson.com.

Company and product names mentioned herein are the trademarks or registered trademarks of their respective owners.

All rights reserved. No part of this book may be reproduced, in any form or by any means, without permission in writing from the publisher.

Printed in the United States of America

Second Printing March 2012

ISBN-10: 0-13-287659-0
ISBN-13: 978-0-13-287659-9

Pearson Education LTD.
Pearson Education Australia PTY, Limited.
Pearson Education Singapore, Pte. Ltd.
Pearson Education Asia, Ltd.
Pearson Education Canada, Ltd.
Pearson Educación de Mexico, S.A. de C.V.
Pearson Education—Japan
Pearson Education Malaysia, Pte. Ltd.

Library of Congress Cataloging-in-Publication Data

Graham, Stedman.

Identity : your passport to success / Stedman Graham.

p. cm.

Includes index.

ISBN 978-0-13-287659-9 (hardcover : alk. paper)

1. Identity (Philosophical concept) 2. Success. I. Title.

BD236.G72 2012

158.1--dc23

2011050616

I dedicate this book to Oprah, who is where she is because she's always known who she was. Thank you for being a teacher in my life. You have made it possible for me to transform and to make a difference in other people's lives throughout the world.

To my daughter Wendy—I appreciate your insights, personal feedback, and support of your dad.

To my sister Anita, the Grahams, the Jacobs, and to the Spaulding Family descendants—Your leadership and support have given me the strength to keep on keeping on.

I dedicate this book to the people who are too many to name, who have impacted my life, and who I have learned from. I am grateful and thankful. This book on identity is the cornerstone and foundation of my potential. It is my vision to share this message and philosophy with people all over the world.

God is love.

Contents

Acknowledgments

I would like to thank Jan Miller for representing me throughout the years as my publishing agent. I appreciate your belief in me and my work. I could not have a better advocate. I also want to thank Shannon, a member of Jan's team, for her tireless work and commitment to this project.

Stewart Emery, thank you for your ideas, thoughts, writing, and assistance on this book. You are among the most talented anywhere. Thank you also to Russ Hall for your gift of understanding my voice.

I appreciate Tim Moore of Pearson Education for his ability to make things happen and for his editing and exceptional skills that have made many projects like this successful.

I appreciate the ongoing work and commitment Kristin Andress has made to this project and many others. It has been a pleasure to have worked with you throughout the years.

A special thank you to my support team: LeVette Straughter, Nadia Estrada, Valera Yazell, Paula Collins, and Amanda Garcia.

About the Author

Stedman Graham is Chairman and CEO of S. Graham & Associates, a management, marketing, and consulting firm based in Chicago, Illinois. Graham speaks, conducts seminars, and develops programs for businesses and educational organizations worldwide. He is the author of ten books, including two *New York Times* bestsellers, *You Can Make It Happen—A Nine-Step Plan for Success* and *Teens Can Make It Happen—Nine Steps to Success*, which illustrate his proprietary Nine-Step Success Process™, a life management and learning system that teaches you how to organize your personal and professional life around your identity.

Foreword
by John C. Maxwell

I have been a student of personal growth, leadership, and success for more than forty years. I believe that having a learner's mindset is very important to that process. You're never too old or too experienced to learn something new. And one of the most important truths about personal growth and success is that you must change yourself first if you want to change your world.

When I met Stedman Graham, I could tell he had a similar outlook. He is a learner. Over the course of time, he has developed a way of approaching life and profession that he has distilled into his Nine-Step Success Process™. It has helped him, and now he is sharing it because he believes it can also help you.

Stedman and I share many of the same approaches to growth and success. You must know yourself to get on the right track. You need strong values, such as integrity, a positive attitude, and a strong work ethic. You must build a team. And you must be willing to keep changing and growing.

In this book, Stedman includes many wonderful stories and insights gained from talking to successful people. These will help you greatly. But what I like most is Stedman's desire to encourage you and to tell you that you can do this! It doesn't matter what your background was. It doesn't matter what your circumstances are. You can do things to positively influence what your future will be.

So enjoy this book. And may it be a passport for your continuing journey of success.

John C. Maxwell,
New York Times Bestselling Author and Leadership Expert

Introduction

"Your time is limited,
so don't waste it living someone else's life."
—Steve Jobs

Have you ever thought about the connection between knowing who you are and achieving success? Have you ever felt unsure of where you fit in the world? Or maybe you were never sure to begin with.

You might think you have a pretty good handle on who you are, your identity. But here's the thing: Most people really don't. And even if you do, your identity can change, evolve, and transform. It's up to you to fully grasp your identity and use it to your advantage to succeed.

If you ask a lot of people who they are, you'll get a host of answers: "I'm a student." "I'm a future CEO in the making." "I'm a single mom." "I'm a Chicago Bulls fan." Others might say, "I like the Yankees." "I'm a Pisces." "I'm a caring, giving person." Some might even admit, "I'm a taker." Whatever the snapshot, it's not a fully developed picture for most people, so you and I are going to take a journey to find out more about identity, and why knowing yours better can be a huge asset.

Although the pages that follow include stories about other people's journeys to success and offer different points of view on how to go about it, this book is really all about you.

As you read, I ask that you think about how what you read applies to you and the life you are creating. Consider how you can put what you read to work for you. Putting the principles you learn into practice will help you build a wonderful life for yourself. As you get further along in this book, you will deeply examine what being successful means, especially for you. For the moment, think of success as the end result of becoming clear about your identity, discovering what you love to do, and learning how to do it really well so you create value in the world.

The core idea of the book is this: Your happiness and success in life flow from becoming clear about who you are and establishing your authentic identity—first inside yourself and then externally in the world.

There is a distinction between the reality of knowing yourself and that of having created a fully functional identity. Knowing yourself is the foundation for building identity. Knowing yourself—being comfortable in your own skin—is an inner process that's not readily observable by others.

Interestingly, however, other people often experience the process because they feel more at ease in the company of a person who is comfortable in his or her own skin. As you become comfortable with who you are, other people will be drawn to you and bring you great opportunity.

You can also think of identity as your personal brand. When painters sign paintings, they are establishing their personal brand; it's their way of saying that what they've done matters. The same goes for authors. My name is on this book. It's there not as a boast—lots of people have written books—but as a sign that part of my identity includes the willingness to reach out and help others. That's something about which I can feel a healthy pride.

You can also think of identity as your personal brand.

In this sense, being clear about your identity is a significant next step beyond knowing who you are and being comfortable in your own skin. Building your identity is about knowing what your calling is, learning how to do it well, and creating value in the world. I've learned that, for the most part, extraordinary people are simply ordinary people doing extraordinary things that matter to them. They relentlessly align all the elements of their life to support their pursuit of what has deep meaning to them. The message here is that you have the ability within you to live an extraordinary life. You have the choice to embrace a personally meaningful journey, integrating your personal and

> *Building your identity is about knowing what your calling is, learning how to do it well, and creating value in the world.*

professional life in ways that make a lasting difference to you and the people around you.

I started to make real progress in my own life when I realized that the American free enterprise system was relevant to every single person. I was five years into my own change process when I realized, "Wow, this is the greatest gift somebody can get as a human being—it doesn't get any better." I said, "Oh, my goodness, that's the freedom." I realized that, everywhere in the world, there are 24 hours in the day, and the process for becoming successful is the same for everybody. It doesn't make any difference what your race is, what your family circumstances are, where you came from, what you look like, what your religion is, what your gender is—the process works the same way. And then I started to buy into the process. I said, "There is a process I can learn and use to build my identity and become successful!" And you can learn it, too. Use your 24 hours wisely. I'll show you how.

In my years of supporting people in their quest for success and freedom, I've also learned that relying on information can be a trap. In a totally connected world, there's no shortage of information. Anyone with an Internet-enabled device has universal access to information overload. But do you feel any clearer about your identity as a result? Most of the people I ask answer, "Not so much." When you've established your identity, you'll be able to sift through information to select the golden nuggets that support you in the pursuit of your dream.

If you don't have an identity, you don't have a choice. You're like a jukebox in the corner. Somebody strolls over, drops in a few quarters, presses a button, and you play their tune. You have no choice. But it doesn't have to be that way. I offer you a gift: the freedom of choice.

Personal growth requires inspirational experiences that move your heart. Way, way back before the Internet began—before there were books, even—the kind of experiences I am talking about began at the feet of the storyteller. With this in mind as I prepared to write this book, I talked to people and collected true stories about them and their journeys to know themselves, to sort out their values, define their identity, and express their voice in the world. Some of them struggled—sometimes a lot.

A number of folks I talked with asked that I not use their names or the names of the people they mentioned, out of respect for other people's privacy. My publisher, Tim Moore, suggested that we engage a writer he knew to turn these particular conversations into short stories, and that is what we have done.

In the following chapters, you will meet a man named Rob and a collection of his friends who all live in a Midwestern town we called Blakenfield. The stories are true. Only the names and location have been changed to protect people's privacy.

CHAPTER 1

You Have a Choice

When I was growing up as one of six children (two of whom were disabled) in Whitesboro, New Jersey, a small black community surrounded by a predominately white community, the catch-phrase was, "Nothing good ever comes out of Whitesboro."

My childhood was tough at times. My two disabled brothers seemed to get all the attention, and as a kid, I didn't know how to deal with that. I was also teased, and my family was called names. I felt a lot of shame through all of this. People put labels on me and called me by those labels—some linked to my disabled brothers, some race-based. So, I had this internal fight going on as I resisted labeling myself, but still wondered, "What if I am?" That led to negative feelings, and I found myself struggling with another fight as I wrestled with my negativity and my anger. That's how my low self-esteem and lack of self-confidence kicked in: I was trying to deal with my feelings but I didn't know how. Thinking about race started to take up a lot of space in my head and left me trying to function with a race-based consciousness, which is what I had.

With a race-based consciousness, every day I woke up thinking I couldn't make it because of the color of my skin. This was tied directly to my self-esteem, my belief systems, my habits, my vision, and my hopes and dreams. It was also directly linked to what I thought my talent was and what skills I thought I could develop. I had a totally self-limiting consciousness.

Picture this: I was a young 6-foot-6 black guy. What did everyone say I was? A basketball player. Label. So I was that. I lived the label. I went on to Abilene, Texas, where I played basketball for Hardin-Simmons University, and then to Ball State University in Muncie, Indiana, for grad school. There I was exposed to many good people, but I also bought into what others said and how others acted instead of getting better in-tune with my own soul. My self-esteem was too low for me to appreciate life. As I once told Mike Kiley of the *Chicago Tribune,* "I was an angry person. I was angry at the system, and I felt a victim in my own right. It was almost as if I had a hole in my heart."

I was a young 6-foot-6 black guy. What did everyone say I was? A basketball player. So I was that. I lived the label.

Then one day, it hit me. It wasn't about race; it was about me not knowing who I was and not having a process for becoming successful. I didn't know how successful people think and act. I'd been told it was about race. I suddenly realized that somebody had fed me a bill of goods, and I had bought into it. And if I'd bought into the notion that it was about race, there was no way out—I would be trying to solve what the problem wasn't.

Later in life, I faced the issue of being Oprah Winfrey's partner. I heard myself referred to as "Oprah's boyfriend" and saw the handiwork of the tabloid media on display at the newsstands. It would have been easy for me to feel like I was really a nobody by having to live in the shadow of the lies they printed. I don't like being in that kind of limelight.

I didn't know how to deal with all of this. And I would never have known how to deal with it had I not learned something else that could replace it—a knowledge of how the free enterprise system worked and a process for becoming successful. I realized that other people had become successful in the system, that they were making money and creating opportunities and making things happen. I knew I didn't know how to do this. I didn't even know how to define it, or what it looked like, or what it consisted of, or how much work was involved. So I had to learn to cope, and I studied and I discussed; I watched and I learned. Now I know how much work is involved, because after my time in the U.S. Army and work in the prison system, I've been in business or running a business. Working in the prison system, I saw what happens to people who don't have a healthy identity or a process for success.

What I came up with is something that has helped me a great deal—and it can help you, too. It's a process for developing your identity, improving your life, and becoming successful.

The usual case is that you're not in a position to be able to improve your life because you haven't been taught a process for doing this. You don't know what to build or don't even realize that you have to build a foundation for your life. You don't have a starting process for living and improving and developing your life because you were taught to go to school, memorize, take tests, repeat the information, and forget it. Then you were stuck in a box doing the same thing over and over every single day. So you had no identity workshop development opportunities. Nobody came to you and said, "Let's work on your identity today." Instead, the external world just kind of took over and said, "Well, if you're not going to spend time on yourself and invest in yourself to develop some self-awareness about your own identity, I'll just take over. I'm going to supply you with music, games, food, chores, a job, and all the other things that take up your life—especially labels for pigeon-holing you." You felt that life was acting upon you instead of feeling like you were in control. You became a worker instead of a thinker. You became a follower instead of a leader—a slave, actually.

If you look at the seven billion people in the world, just 1% understand that they are the thinkers—and therefore, they run everything. This is the problem with our society and our country. We have too many people who are not innovative, too many people who are dropping out of school, too many people who have given up their lives, too many people who don't have the skills to reinvent themselves, too many people looking for jobs who aren't able to control their own destinies. They feel that life is controlling them and that they have no control over it.

You may feel the same. Look, it's not just you. When I started to figure out that a key piece was missing in my own life, I was about 32 or 33. That's when I realized that I didn't know who I was, and I didn't understand the value of an education. I thought, "Man, you need a new education—and you need to wake up!"

I didn't know who I was, and I didn't understand the value of an education.

Just as you may be, I got very frustrated and built up a lot of anger—a lot of rage. The thing that saved me in high school was basketball. Being a 1,000-point scorer on the high school team was a boost. Basketball helped me develop enough confidence in myself not to destroy myself with all of the negative energy I had built up inside. You've got two sides of the equation: assets and liabilities. Your success is based on your assets versus your liabilities. Now, how many liabilities do you have standing in the way of assets that you can create in your life? Positive versus negative, good versus bad, love versus hate. It's all the same stuff.

What tipped the switch for me was the fact that, by my early thirties, I had a pretty good base. I'd played basketball in

Europe and I'd traveled around. I'd been in the U.S. Army, which helped me create some structure. I was building strength. I was looking for the structure because it was structure I needed. Then I worked in the prison system for five years, and that also provided structure. Some of us rebel against any form of structure, but that doesn't mean we don't need it. It was my good fortune to understand that I needed it.

As I think back to my time in high school again, I realize I was pretty active. I was a drum major in the band, I played basketball, and I was active in a lot of clubs. I had a great support system in church and little league baseball—all that kind of stuff. So to be fair, I had a lot of strength coming in, despite the fact that I was dealing with a lot of other stuff I felt to be negative. It was like an internal contest of good thinking versus bad thinking. I had to weigh all of that. I didn't have a process for doing this—to get out of my own bad dream.

If you feel you have no control over your life, you need to come to the same epiphany I did, that, "Oh, I'm not alone." Millions of women buy into the belief that they can't make it because they're a woman. Where I came from, people of color buy into the belief that they can't make it because of the color of their skin. That's their label. I'm not alone. Folks who think that they're entitled because they're a certain race, that because they're white they're better than somebody else, they are labeled. They buy into that. Or maybe you think that you can't succeed because your mother or father told you that you're nothing and that you're never going to be anything.

So you've got all these labels. I realized that I'm not the only person around here with a label. And I realized that the secret to unlabeling yourself is not to let other people define you. You need to define yourself—and you can, *if you know how*.

And I realized that the secret to unlabeling yourself is not to let other people define you. You need to define yourself—and you can, if you know how.

That's why I created the Nine-Step Success Process, a structure that you can follow in everything you do. It will get you results and performance in business as well as personal life. But you've got to be clear—you've got to have clarity, you've got to have focus, you've got to have alignment, you've got to have repetition, you've got to have skills, you've got to have information, and you've got to have improvement in your own internal life so that you can build your foundation. Then you'll able to expand that into the larger world and pull out what you need in order to succeed on a larger scale.

Traditional learning in this world works the opposite of how you actually should learn. You've basically learned to be a worker. The world wants workers. So the educational system teaches you how to be a worker, how to get a job, and how to prepare yourself so you can go out and do the work. You're programmed to basically do the same thing over and over every day. If you buy into this, you get trapped because you get comfortable with the status quo. Without intervention or without some consciousness telling you that you need to do more than what you're doing, you're not going to do it. It's impossible. You're certainly not going to do it if you're trained not to do it—or if you don't train yourself.

You need intervention, and that's what I'm providing through this book. I'm coming into your life and saying, "You need to wake up. You've been sleeping." The majority of people in many communities just loll along and act as if they've been hypnotized. They don't have any kind of goals; they don't have a vision. They may have a daily goal that they want to achieve today, but it's the same goal they had yesterday. Same thing, same thing, same thing. There's no process for continuous improvement. There's no journey. Where are you going? Where are you going to be in five years? Where are you going to be in ten years? What are you going to create in your life?

Most people don't know they can do that. They don't even know they can create a vision. They don't even know what a vision is. Why? Because schools don't teach vision. So I created a process that I could follow to reinvent myself, brand myself, and rebrand myself consistently. I needed a structure because I work best through structure, and I work through processes. When I discovered the benefit of process, I realized, "Oh, we have all of these things we don't do because there's no process for getting them done." So I started to organize every part of my life and put that into a process, to build value. I realized, "This is about talent and skills. This is about performance. It's about creating value." And that's way beyond the entitlement mentality of, "What is the world going to do for me?" The structure I'm talking about is, "How can I go out there and create value?"

You want value. That's the key. It doesn't matter whether you're living in an affluent section of Chicago or you're living in poverty in a Chicago housing project. The question is, how do you get beyond where you are? How do you do something more than what you're doing? What kind of process can you develop? What can you do to enhance your value as a human being?

You have the potential to find value if you understand the process. I had to figure it out. I watched Oprah and what she's accomplished and realized that what she has comes from an internal base. She had a different kind of thinking. We were searching for the same thing, but she found it early. She knew there was a difference. She was also smarter, brighter. She was able to process. I didn't have the process. I probably could have gotten it earlier if I'd been a different kind of a thinker, but I didn't understand the value of process and good thinking. I just wasn't as good a thinker.

So, what's a thinker? A thinker is someone who is conscious. A thinker is someone who has intent—someone who has a methodology to put things together. A thinker has been taught to think and also has self-awareness. A thinker is inquisitive, thinks in detail, and can actually put things together based on how things work. Who's taught that—who's trained to think? We don't teach people to think. But I'm going to try to help you do just that.

One of the key points I stress in this book is your understanding of the difference between the internal world and the external one. As I've said, this book is all about you. You're going to make your own discoveries, aided by your observations from the stories I present. I use stories because people are moved by other people's experiences. There's no transformation in mere information, though.

You have to focus if you are to get sustainable benefits from this. Focus is huge. Once you lose your focus, it's tough. You're all over the place. You have no focus? You'd better get some focus, and then figure out what you're going to do repeatedly over a period of time. That's the only way you can create excellence. You can't create excellence any other way—and if you don't create excellence, how are you going to be an independent learner or thinker? How are you going to get beyond the system if you don't have some brand, if you don't have some base, if you don't have some foundation that separates you from everybody else? It all goes back to what I was talking about, which is value. How in the world is somebody going to give you value or respect if you don't stand for something? The most important point is that you have a choice. You can decide to be a leader or be a victim. It's all up to you.

Think you're not worthy? That's the biggest bunch of hog-wash in the world. You've got the same opportunity I have. You just don't believe that you have it. You just don't believe enough in yourself to be able to take advantage of it. You're afraid you might succeed, and then you can't live with that because you've been beating yourself up all your life. You may be conditioned based on that mindset, but you can break free from it.

The most important point is that you have a choice. You can decide to be a leader or be a victim. It's all up to you.

I want you to understand that this is an internal journey. Once you go external, you'd better know what you're doing. Once you get out in the world, the world will hurt you if you're not prepared. So I'm trying to help you transform your thinking from weakness to strength. You've got to become strong. You've got to believe in yourself, to be motivated about you. You've got to focus on you. Without you, nothing works. Don't worry about whether or not somebody cares about you. Instead, say, "I'm going to take charge of my own life, because if I wait on the world to do it for me, I'm in trouble."

The first step in the journey to freedom and success is to check your ID. That's not as easy as it sounds, but it's doable. If I defined it formally, I would say your identity is based on your passions, on what you love. It includes being clear about your values and how you personally define success for yourself. It's worthwhile to ask about your personal definition of identity. It's different for everyone, but you may already have some idea about what it is. You may not know how to make the most of it or how to use it in a way that empowers you. Or you may feel that you have a weak or not fully formed identity. Or maybe you'd like to trade in the identity you have for a different one. Even when you've established your understanding of your identity, your job isn't done. You have to redefine yourself constantly. It's the constant reinvention of yourself that determines how you begin to create your image or brand. It's about constant improvement, constant revision, constant learning.

I've been teaching and writing about a Nine-Step Success Process for a long time. Along the way, I've come to see that, unless the person taking these nine steps is well on the way to knowing who he or she is and possesses an identity driven by vision and defined by values, the journey to success usually doesn't end well. Nonetheless, these steps are important, and you can follow them with confidence as you start doing the work to know yourself and define your identity.

I refer back to these steps throughout the book.

NINE-STEP SUCCESS PROCESS

Step 1. **Check Your ID**—Explore your identity. Find out who you really are. Success depends upon self-awareness.

Step 2. **Create Your Vision**—A well-defined vision enables you to make meaningful, realistic goals for your business or personal life.

Step 3. **Develop Your Travel Plan**—Create a plan of action that allows you to work toward your goals.

Step 4. **Master the Rules of the Road**—You need guidelines to keep you on track, such characteristics as honesty, trust, hard work, determination, and a positive attitude.

Step 5. **Step into the Outer Limits**—Make the leap. To grow, you have to leave your comfort zone. Remember, risk is a natural part of life; staying the same is standing still, and change (growth) means risk.

Step 6. **Pilot the Seasons of Change**—If you keep doing what you've always done, you'll get the same results.

Step 7. **Build Your Dream Team**—Build supportive relationships with mentors and peers who can help you toward your goals.

Step 8. **Win by a Decision**—What you are in this world is the result of the decisions you've made so far in your life. The choices you make now will be one of your greatest challenges. Consider carefully how they will impact your personal life, family, profession and career, and, of course, your long-term vision.

Step 9. **Commit to Your Vision**—Put all your energy and effort into achieving your goals. Enthusiasm and commitment generate excellence, and that leads to success. The challenge is to develop the ability to coexist with the world as it changes, never giving in and never giving up.

QUESTIONS TO CONSIDER

You might ask how it can be possible to know more about yourself than you already do, but in truth very few people know themselves as they might. This probably includes you. When Socrates said, "The unexamined life isn't worth living," this is what he was talking about. Take a deep, hard look at fascinating you. Examine your life. So, where to start?

1. You can often learn a lot about a character in a book or movie by what he or she wants. What do you want, desire, or crave in your life? Do you have a passion that drives you? Are you a fan? Do you have hobbies? What's on your bucket list? What dream makes you, well, you?

   ____

   ____

   ____

2. Consider where you are on any number of sliding scales—at the left, at the right, or somewhere in the middle. Are you an introvert or extrovert, quiet or loud, humorous or humorless, class clown or A student, a dog person or a cat person, a giver or a taker, honest or devious, a self-starter or someone who needs direction, a listener or a talker, a leader or a follower, a spiritual person or a secular one, and on and on.

   ____

   ____

   ____

3. Take a hard look at your personal values. Write them down. How do they look on paper? Do you value honesty, reliability, patience, or something else?

____

____

____

4. Get close but candid friends to give you an honest assessment. How do they picture your identity? What do they perceive your values to be? Is there a difference between the way you perceive yourself and the way others perceive you?

____

____

____

5. Consider your history and setting. Where did you grow up? How are your family members and friends part of your identity? Are you content with the way you are and where you're headed, or is this a starting place toward somewhere else?

____

____

____

6. Think about whether knowing more about your identity helps you focus on the people you want to be around, where you want to go in your life, what you desire, and what you value most. Has this process changed any of your goals or modified your understanding of what success and a richer life means for you?

____

____

____

7. Are there any labels you have for yourself? Do others know you by certain labels? Are they fair, proper, and do you deserve them, or are they like shackles from which you should shake free?

____

____

____

C H A P T E R 2

Knowing Yourself Should Be Easy. It Isn't. Why Is That?

This is the first of our stories set in Blakenfield, a fictitious town in the Midwest. All the people in this book are real, as are their stories. As I mentioned in the Introduction, the people in these stories asked that we change their names and locations, to respect their privacy.

Carol was the hardest-working person Rob had ever seen at the Blakenfield Gym. She was there every day, sometimes twice a day. Her tanned skin glistened with a sheen of sweat as she attacked the elliptical machine, the ponytail of her long blond hair flying from side to side as steady as a metronome, except for the stray lock stuck to her moist forehead. As soon as she toweled off from that, she was on to free weights with her personal trainer, Matt, who happened to be the gym owner and manager. After that, she might take an aerobics class or a 5-mile jog. But when she really kicked into high gear, she worked out alone in the aerobics room when it was empty. Definitely driven by something, mused Rob.

When he'd first seen her, Rob hadn't immediately thought her to be beautiful. Up close, though, he'd been struck by her generous lips and her eyes that threw sparkling spears, along with a grace that hinted of jaguar. He'd seen a jaguar at a zoo, restless and pacing in its too-small a cage. There was some of that to Carol, too—the grace, the pride, the dignity, and the constrained energy of someone who was ready to run full out across the savannah. Definitely beautiful, he decided, in a classic kind of way. She could stand there radiating warmth while showing almost no expression at all, as if she'd taught herself not to frown or even smile too much in order to prevent wrinkles from forming on her smooth, perfect skin.

But then there was that cage. He sensed a hunger, or at least some yearning, within her. It was as if she was longing for something more.

He sensed a hunger, or at least some yearning, within her. It was as if she was longing for something more.

Rob knew that Carol's husband, Bane Richards, the biggest contractor in their hometown of Blakenfield, Illinois, had put up dozens of developments and strip malls. He drove a big black pickup truck, smoked cigars, and spoke of his wife as "the little lady." Rob had heard Carol describe trips where Bane took groups of people on shindigs to Las Vegas or New Orleans, riding in limos and drinking the best champagne. But when Carol talked about her husband, her stories had a noticeable lack of bubbles. She'd had enough of that life and spoke with neither passion nor joy. She had always lived in his shadow. The wives of Bane's golfing buddies weren't that friendly to Carol, either, Rob knew. She was just the younger wife—a bit of a trophy, but not for first place, as far as they were concerned. Her only time in the spotlight came in her visits to the gym, where her intensity both amused and intimidated everyone around her.

Rob watched Carol on the stationary bike once, pumping faster and faster, setting the controls for hills until she was on a course that could have prepped her for *Le Tour de France.* He asked her once if she'd ridden far enough to cross the state line. She said, "At least." As she pumped at the pedals, he wouldn't have been surprised to see the bike pop off its stand and shoot out the gym door. Again he wondered what drove her.

"What in the world motivates you, Carol?" Rob asked.

"Oh, I just like to be fit." She shared a Mona Lisa smile—her signature one, with a wry twist to the corner of her mouth—that was in stark contrast to the grimace she often wore as she hoisted dumbbells and did countless crunches.

This was the only gym in Blakenfield, and Carol stood out as the hardest working of its patrons. Blakenfield was the kind of Midwestern town where people knew each other, or thought they did. Some grew up and moved away, only to come back later. Some lived there all their lives. It was a goldfish bowl, or narrow cage, and everyone could both look in and look out. Carol had grown up in the weave of that fabric and played by its rules. If she was frustrated by life, she kept it mostly to herself and spun any dreams she might have by pounding her hard body into perfect form with one exercise after another. This home-away-from-home could be the only place she was happy. The one time she'd brought her teenage son to the gym—he'd been grounded, something about a wreck and not having a license—the boy sprawled in an awkward, sullen slump in the corner, like a load of wet clothes waiting to go into the dryer. He merely stared at his black fingernails in pouty boredom as he waited on one of her usual long and intensive workouts to end.

Rob suspected there was more to what drove her than just being fit. That proved to be the case when he heard Carol had separated from her husband—and all the financial security that went with that arrangement. Her son had stayed with his father. Carol had moved into a small apartment and taken a job at the gym. She made just enough to get by—and her workouts became more intense than ever.

In her one-on-one workouts with Matt, her personal trainer, it was hard to miss the way she looked at him, or that she sometimes went to watch when Matt played tennis or basketball at the park. Carol was enough older than Matt that his sports buddies sometimes kidded him about having his mom watch his games. Matt shrugged it off, but Rob saw something in Carol's eyes that hinted she had grown a strong emotional attachment to Matt. Was she acting out transference and hunger?

One day Carol wasn't at the gym. That was odd. Rob asked around and got the story. She'd been in a traffic accident. She'd been driving and was on the side of the car that got hit. She was in critical condition. Her best friend, Lisbeth, had escaped with shock and noncritical injuries.

A group of gym members chipped in for a fruit basket, and Rob went along when they visited the hospital. They were let into a room where Lisbeth was still under observation. She had a nondisplaced fracture of the collarbone—caused by the seat belt, she said—and she'd been banged up a bit. A bruise on her forehead was dark purple. Rob could only imagine how Carol looked.

"We tried to see Carol, too," Rob said, "but the nurse says she doesn't want to see anyone."

"She's working through some things," Lisbeth said, her lips pressed into a tight line.

"What happened?" Rob asked.

"It was strange." Lisbeth tilted her head and looked up at the corner or the room, as if seeing everything again on a screen there. "We were sitting at a light on our way to grab dinner. Carol was driving. She wanted to talk about how attracted she was to Matt. She'd told him, but he'd made it clear he didn't want to play that game. I had my head down, typing a text message. I heard her touch the gas, felt the car start to accelerate forward. I looked up and could see the lights were still red. My head snapped toward her. It wasn't like she looked mad and was doing something on purpose. Not suicidal—just not there. Her face was calm, perfect as a picture—no expression at all, no eagerness, no fear, but kind of spaced out. Just past her, I could see a pickup coming as fast as it could to make it through the yellow light. I felt and heard the crash, felt us being crunched and spun and toppled clear over. Then I was out of it until I came to at the hospital."

"And Carol? Is she...okay? Did you get to see her?" Rob wished he hadn't spoken almost as soon as the words were out.

Lisbeth turned her head. Her lips quivered. "Yes, I saw her."

Rob and his friends looked at each other, but none of them thought of anything more to say or ask. Soon they were heading out of the antiseptic-smelling hallways and out into the fresh air, and Rob realized they didn't know very much about what had happened to Carol.

A couple weeks later, Lisbeth showed up at the gym. She was pumping away on a stationary bicycle without moving her shoulders much. Rob went over to her. "Have you gotten to see Carol lately?"

"Yep." She frowned as she looked over the handlebars at him. "Not pretty."

"Will she be...all right?"

"Depends on what you mean by that. One foot was crushed beyond saving and had to be amputated above the ankle. Her chest had caved in. She's endured three operations so far, and the plastic surgeon hasn't even started on her face."

"Her face?" Rob could see that clear, shining skin, so devoid of anything even close to a wrinkle.

"Yeah." Lisbeth shook her head. "Not good. Not good at all."

Rob thought of Carol often after that. He could still see her healthy and complete body spinning in cartwheels across that aerobics mat. No one talked in detail about the extent of her injuries, but Rob recalled the words *amputation* and *plastic surgeon* and *face*. Not good.

Whenever he saw Lisbeth after that and asked about Carol, for a long time she just shook her head. Rob couldn't imagine that what Carol was going through could be pleasant, and he was feeling bad about not reaching out to her directly. He simply had no idea how to be with someone in Carol's situation. He wasn't sure he could handle it.

Then one day when Rob asked Lisbeth about Carol again, she smiled and shared a warm glow of inner happiness. "You know, Carol has finally started to go at her rehab with the same intensity she used to show at the gym. She's coming along better than expected, and even though the plastic surgeries haven't done all she'd hoped, she's starting to show signs of life again. In fact, in some ways, she seems more alive than I've ever seen her."

"Really?"

"You just wait and see," Lisbeth said. "She's going to start back to work again, right here at this gym."

"She's not too embarrassed about the thing with Matt?"

"If it bothered her before, it doesn't seem to now."

A few weeks after he'd spoken with Lisbeth, Rob came to the gym and saw Carol back at work. She was behind the desk when he came in, but when she came out around the desk to escort a prospective patron, Rob saw that she wore shorts, with her prosthetic lower leg there for everyone to see. The plastic surgeries hadn't entirely fixed her face. One corner of her mouth twisted up into a puckered cheek that reminded Rob distantly of the Joker in the *Batman* movie. But if looking in the many mirrors at the gym bothered Carol at all, she sure didn't show it. That amazed Rob. What a lot of spunk that took! She smiled more, too—she seemed more alive somehow and didn't seem to care now whether she got smile wrinkles.

For a while, Rob still walked on eggshells around Carol, careful of what he said and asked. But there was that persistent smile, more genuine than ever. The spunky, wry twist to her mouth was more pronounced than ever, and her eyes still glittered. So one day, he approached her at the gym's juice bar, where she was cleaning and cutting up pomegranates and bananas. She had washed a batch of blueberries and squeezed fresh oranges and limes.

"How are you doing, Carol?"

"Ah." She looked up with a laughing smile. "What you're really wondering is how I can come back and work in the same place as Matt. Isn't that right?"

Rob started to frown but instead gave her a slow nod.

"Well, have you ever heard of people who have to rush out of their homes in the face of fires, hurricanes, or floods? They grab only what matters to them. It's a real cold-water splash in the face about what you value—and what you don't. I've gotten clear about what really matters to me. I've had a lot of time to reflect on who I was. Starting out, I didn't think I was anybody who mattered. I didn't matter to my father, as far as I could tell. He'd wanted a son. When I was a little girl, if I made mistakes reading, he would push me off his lap and tell me I was stupid and would never amount to anything on my own. He'd say it was a good thing I was pretty and that I'd better find a successful man to take care of me. I remember all the times he would turn away from me and leave the room when I came home from school—even after I found out I was dyslexic, not stupid. It hurt. And you know, I went and did what he told me: I used my looks and my body to catch a successful man to take care of me. But then I found out I was caught, too, and it felt like I was paying a terrible price. I thought I would feel good if I left my husband and went out on my own. It only worked for a little while. Then I just felt all alone and empty inside, almost like I was disappearing.

"After the accident, I was blessed with a wonderful social worker as part of my rehab. She helped me understand what it meant to become my own person, to stop trying to be what I thought other people wanted me to be. She'd look at me and gently laugh, and tell me now would be a good time to find out there was more to me than my looks.

"I didn't bounce back right away. I seemed to go down and down a dark hole for quite a while there. I'd never been depressed in my life, especially for so long. I tried to tell myself there were people worse off in the world, who were starving, or having their families wiped out by wars, or being hurt in far worse ways than me. I'd get mad at myself for being so sad, and then I'd yell at myself and scream. 'Are you crying?' I'd yell. 'What's wrong with you?' I'd try to shame myself out of my blue funk. Of course, this didn't work, either. I'd look at the bottle of pain pills and a bottle of tequila and think about overdosing. Can't tell you why I didn't—but I didn't.

"I felt myself stewing in this pool of, well, anger. This just made me feel more frustrated. I was being abused, but by myself! Then I got to a really quiet place, the land of apathy. Nothing mattered anymore. I didn't matter to the world, and the world didn't matter to me. I couldn't feel anything. On the other hand, nothing could hurt me here. And you know, that was kind of liberating. I'd ask, 'What do you want?' and I had no answer. I'd ask it again and again and again. Then one

Nothing mattered anymore. I didn't matter to the world, and the world didn't matter to me. I couldn't feel anything.

rainy day, when I should have been as low as the old socks in the bottom of my sock drawer, I suddenly could answer the question. 'I want to matter,' I said. 'I want to be able to do something the way all the people did who helped me when I was drifting away from life. They knew I could come around, and eventually, with their respect and love, I did. I want to make a difference like that,' I said. 'I want to matter like that.' From that point on, it was only upward."

"Wow," was all Rob could say.

She said, "You know something, Rob? I feel more alive and full of purpose than I ever have been. All I've been through has opened my eyes to what's important. I was living the unexamined life, addicted to appearances. But sooner or later, age was going to kick my butt on that ride. I was sure on a slippery slope. But now I'm finding myself much more connected to others, and I'm starting to really care about what matters to them. I'm learning about values and what it means to lead a life filled with purpose. I find myself drawn to people who share my values. For the first time in my life, I feel real—and that I matter.

"The main thing is," she said, "I feel I'm really starting to know who I am. I thought I knew before, but I was wrong. I'd let everybody but me decide who I was or should be. Now I'm working this out for myself, and I'm getting closer. And I kind of like what I've discovered so far. Some mornings I look in the mirror and feel that I really like the person I see there, slightly broken face and all."

"And what's this new you going to do with her life?" Rob asked.

"My social worker has enrolled me in a career college and has become my mentor," she said. "I'm going to go to school to be a child and family counselor. Who knows? I may even come to understand my own teenage son! As part of the program, I'll be counseling other people who need someone to be there for them and care about them just the way they are, while helping them do better in life. I'm excited about all of this. I want to help people the way people helped me and saved my life. I wouldn't wish what I went through on anyone, but if that's what it takes for me to learn to admire what others do, what purpose drives them, then so be it. I'm going to succeed on my own terms and do some good at the same time."

I'd let everybody but me decide who I was or should be. Now I'm working this out for myself, and I'm getting closer.

Rob took a good look at her. In a way, that almost perfect Barbie-like appearance she'd once had wasn't half as beautiful as how she looked now, even with an artificial leg and that unusual twist to her smile. Everything about her now was deeper, more real, and more full of purpose. He saw new dimensions in her—something he'd never seen before—a confidence, he realized, that hadn't been there previously.

STEP #1—CHECK YOUR ID

Becoming self-aware of who you really are is a vital step in achieving dreams and goals. You need to know what you value, what you want, and the driving principles that make you who you are. When you know who you truly are, to the very last value, you will feel secure enough to accept the influence of others on your life, and you will be open to love, caring, and helping those around you.

DISCUSSION

When you look in the mirror, you see an individual you should know quite well. Yet most of us don't know that person grinning or smirking back at us as well as we think we do—as well as we should, as well as we could. For Carol, getting to know herself involved a painful and difficult journey to a place in her life where she could look in the mirror and like the person she saw, slightly crooked smile and all.

Try to write a ten-word want ad for yourself—and be honest. (That's the hard part!) Do you end up with an accurate portrait? Or do you end up with something that sounds like someone else, or someone you'd like to be?

Is yours like this:

Loyal, compassionate, hard-working, spiritual person who enjoys invigorating exercise outdoors.

Or is it like this:

Introverted stay-at-home who prefers listening to drain-pipe moanings to conversation, and watching TV to exercise.

Note how the first one focuses on values, and the second one not so much. Or do you even know that much about yourself?

In his *Poor Richard's Almanac*, Ben Franklin wrote, "There are three things extremely hard: steel, a diamond, and to know one's self."

In job interviews, you are asked, "What are your strengths? What are your weaknesses?"

The people you date ask, "What do you like? What don't you like?"

People you meet may ask, "What's the best thing you've ever done?

What's the best thing you've never done, but wish you had?"

All your life you compare and contrast, explore and search. But knowing yourself well is, well, elusive.

When people steal your identity, as we say, they get only numbers—your Social Security number, your home and phone numbers, and (gasp) your bank account number. But you can fix all that, however painful. The thieves may have stolen money, but they haven't touched the real thing of value.

That's because your value is slippery, elusive, and stuck deep inside you, where you have to grapple hard to know what exactly makes you unique—successful...or not, attractive to others...or not.

> *It may seem an easy task for you to know exactly who you are, to know your identity. But it isn't.*

It may seem an easy task for you to know exactly who you are, to know your identity. But it isn't. The biggest reason is people often confuse surface appearances with what really matters—your values, why you do the things you do, what motivates you, and why.

If someone you know at school starts to wear a beret, you know they're seeking to project a new identity. The same goes for someone you always knew as Rob but who suddenly wants everyone to call him Robert. And think about tattoos and piercings—do they really change or add to identity? They're merely surface changes, superficial adjustments. They're simply reflections of identity and an attempt to shape individuality. They are not the real thing.

What are the *real* properties of identity, and how can we recognize them? Some people may say they know perfectly well who they are, but they could be fooled, the way Carol was. What's more, people can change, and then what? Some people spend all their lives trying to pin down their identities, to find out who they truly are, but they can't seem to grasp their identity with both hands. Why is this all so hard, and what can you do about it?

This is not a new issue. In ancient times, Socrates said the first step to everything was to "Know thyself." He went so far as to say that the unexamined life is not worth living. So how do you go about examining yourself, to really get to know yourself? That's what you'll be exploring in the rest of this book.

QUESTIONS TO CONSIDER

1. Are you happy with who you are—with who you think you are? Some people call this being comfortable in your skin.

   ___

   ___

   ___

2. Do you think you project a clear identity to others, either those you know well or those you first meet? Is it a good identity?

   ___

   ___

   ___

3. Are there things you would change about your identity, or wish you could change, or would even have someone else change for you?

   ___

   ___

   ___

Don't worry if you don't have clear answers to everything at this point. And be a little suspicious if you do. It's the nature of identity to be a little elusive. When we dig deep, we often find that the elusive core of identity—who we are and what we can become—depends a lot more on our personal values than we think. So let's discuss, in the next chapter, how values are the real core of our identities.

CHAPTER 3

What Do Your Personal Values Have to Do with Your Identity?

An old Cherokee told his grandson, "My son, there is a battle between two wolves inside us all. One is anger, jealousy, greed, resentment, inferiority, lies, and ego. The other is good. It is joy, peace, love, hope, humility, kindness, empathy, and truth."
The boy thought about it and asked, "Grandfather, which wolf wins?"
The old man quietly replied, "The one you feed."

Rob parked his car in the municipal lot and sighed as he looked at the red-and-brown brick building that contained Blakenfield's city jail. His best friend was in there. Inside. Locked up. Again.

His steps sounded in hollow clicks as he followed the guard down a row of cells. Allen had been moved from the bullpen to a smaller holding area for their chat. The guard stopped outside a cell and said, "You can talk from here." He took a few steps down the hall and waited, leaning back against a solid-looking wall.

Inside, a lanky body bent forward, forearms on knees, like some vulture hovering over a body, until he heard their steps and the guard's voice. The head that snapped up was the sort

Rob might expect to see in a dark night alley: someone caught in the middle of making a crack deal, or a vagrant lifting his head from a dumpster where he'd been digging for food. It showed an odd mix of shame and anger, of confidence and self-pity, and of relief tangled with fear.

Rob could hardly believe this was the bright star of their high school class, the drum major of the band, the valedictorian, the person he'd shared his summers with, and the only alumni of their school ever to attend Harvard on a scholarship.

What squeezed Rob's heart the most was how they'd both grown up believing they'd had such promise, such possibilities. Through Boy Scouts and summer camps together, shooting hoops on weekends, double-dating at prom, and even Rob being best man at Allen's first wedding, they had seen the world as their oyster, there for easy picking, especially when Allen had headed off for the Ivy League.

Allen rose and came closer to the iron bars, moving slowly, as if his bones were fragile. They probably were. He'd been in a car wreck that had broken several bones and, more recently, had fallen out of bed, far from sober, and had shattered a shoulder. That had cost him the last job he'd had—and that had been quite a while ago. He had battled malnutrition by ignoring the need for food. He believed he could find everything he needed in a bottle, and he'd been looking there for it the hard way. Rob had been part of two interventions, but that hadn't kept two marriages from failing. Allen had three children by the two wives, and, he'd almost proudly said to Rob, he'd never paid a penny of child support. He was in jail this time for contempt of court, for failing to get a job.

> *He believed he could find everything he needed in a bottle, and he'd been looking there for it the hard way.*

His longish hair was a tangle of silver unplanned macramé. The matching stubble on his checks, and the rumpled, long-sleeved shirt with a knobby elbow showing through painted a picture that matched the passive outrage, glowering naiveté, and overconfidence rooted in despair. Allen's big Adam's apple bobbed in the stretched, ropey sinews of his forward-thrust neck as he said, "These people have it in for me. No one wants me to succeed."

That wasn't true. Rob had given Allen several thousand dollars to ostensibly save the financial wreck that was Allen's first marriage, but the money had been frittered away, and so had the marriage.

After two bouts of rehab, Rob had helped the second wife track him down to one of a half-dozen favorite haunts where Allen could sit at the bar and regale some stranger with "the time he had gone to Harvard." Nothing Rob had ever said had gotten through. Allen denied he had a problem, and denied it with a drunken slur. It pained Rob to the corners of his own complicated soul to see Allen refuse to seek work, to stumble again and again, and to wave fierce, useless arms at the sky blaming others for the harm he was really doing to himself.

Here was a friend, a pal of his youth, who had held the greatest promise of them all, but he'd squandered it. Worse, Allan could no longer look forward to something he could strive for, to seek to achieve. He could only look back at something that had happened long ago and now had come to matter very little. Rob couldn't figure it out. It made no sense to him, and he had tried everything. Nothing had worked. It was as if Allen's gearshift had gotten stuck at some point, and he couldn't go forward to grow, adapt, change, or even survive on his own. Allen had become someone who hadn't lived up to the responsibility of the commitments to two wives and three children, who hadn't had the honor and dignity to be part of their lives the way a parent should.

"My last ex, well, she's just plain vindictive," Allen said, heating up to the subject.

"Don't you think there are things you could do to learn?" Rob asked. "Places you could work and matter?"

"That's all past me now."

So Rob told Allen about a friend of his who had weathered something worse than Allen was facing. When he got done, he said, "You could do something like that."

The guard tapped his nightstick on the block wall and then tapped the face of his watch. Time was up.

"I don't see it," Allen said. "Not likely."

"There in a nutshell," Rob sighed, "is the problem."

Allen's story is a cautionary tale of what can happen to you when you don't know who you are and don't have a good set of values to live by. This next story is about someone who took a different path, the kind of path that was open to Rob's friend Allen. But of course, Allen just couldn't see it. Here's the story of Jim Keyes.

Profile in Success

Jim Keyes, CEO of Blockbuster

When Netflix rolled into the movie-renting world, with additional competition from Apple, Amazon, and Redbox, a lot of people figured that was it for Blockbuster. But they didn't account for the resilience of Jim Keyes, the scrappy CEO of Blockbuster. Jim says his ability to deal with adversity and to stay the course has a lot to do with his identity.

Far from being born with a silver spoon in his mouth, Jim had a humble beginning. "I was born into a very challenged economic environment," he says. "We lived in a three-room house with no running water; a wood-burning stove in the cold winters of central Massachusetts; and an outdoor pump for access to fresh water." He didn't think of that environment as challenging, though. "I never even thought about being poor, because we were actually, I thought, quite happy, until that came apart when I was five years old." His parents split because his mother had been seeing someone else, and she ended up leaving. "So, I found myself in a situation where, with my mother gone, my father wasn't in any position to take care of me because he was working, trying to make ends meet." Jim ended up staying with his siblings, first with one who had recently married, and then bouncing from family to family, all the while hoping that his parents would get back together or that he could live with his father. Instead, he says, "I had to pretty much take care of myself because he was at work all day. When entering the first grade, I was very much on my own as an independent six-year-old having to fend for myself. I realized at that point that no one was going to be there to take care of me, and if I wasn't able to find out how to get the support from the outside world that I needed, I probably wasn't going to have a very easy time of it."

His life was at a crossroads. One experiment with a homemade rocket had set a field on fire and nearly burned down their small house. The incident could have led him to life as a troublemaker, as some people saw him after the incident. But successes at school taught him the positive power of getting an education. As Jim puts it, "I remember seeing that education was something for which people praised me when I did well. I recognized that there was a correlation between my identity and the way people treated me and my success in school."

I recognized that there was a correlation between my identity and the way people treated me and my success in the school.

That path could have ended when high school did. He admits, "No one in my immediate family had attended college.... Neither of my parents graduated from high school. My brothers and sisters had not gone beyond a high school or trade school education, so there was no expectation that I would go any further."

But one role model did make a difference for him. His Uncle Lenny had taken advantage of the G.I. Bill to get a college degree and had become a teacher in North Adams, Massachusetts. Jim's family visited him every once in a while. "It was an amazing experience, because my other aunts and uncles grew up pretty much the way I did, in very, very poor surroundings. But this uncle actually had a beautiful home. I thought it was a huge house and remember his library, full of books. It inspired me because I equated books with education. I attributed his success, his personal identity, and the dignities that he carried to the education that set him apart from his siblings. I clearly remember the respect that I felt for him as a very young child."

Getting more education and being around people who could help and support him while doing so began to loom as a desirable path. Jim says, "I instinctively recognized as a child that the only way I was going to survive being thrust into the world, pretty much on my own, was to have the support of the greater world outside of my immediate family. Therefore, I took very seriously, early on, the importance of gaining the respect and support of those in the outside world. As early as six or seven years old, I saw that an important step was building a support system around me. The only way I was going to accomplish that

The only way I was going to survive being thrust into the world pretty much on my own was to have the support of the greater world outside of my immediate family.

was to develop a personal identity in terms of the way people interacted with me. I came to realize that a big piece of the success that I had later in life was the ability to develop my own identity at a very early age."

Getting more schooling wasn't easy for someone from a poor family. He admits, "I didn't believe I could afford to go to college. I applied to The College of the Holy Cross, which was close to home, thinking that if I could get in there, I could do it less expensively. I could live at home. It was the best school I could afford to go to without having to pay for room and board." Jim gained early admission and a small baseball scholarship. He worked three different jobs to try to pay for the rest of the expenses his first year.

Once in college, his identity became an issue again. He says, "I was shocked how similar everybody was. They all came from similar backgrounds, with two parents and… money. Most of the other students knew they would be going to college from the time they were born. And here I was very, very different," Jim says. "But I drew from that strength of my identity as a child and thought, you know, my difference is going to make me more interesting. I was never shy about mixing with the rich kids or the few other poor kids who were there. I felt that I had an advantage in my ability to move freely from circle to circle. I felt that the kids who grew up privileged didn't have the same kind of confidence, socially, in mixing with others who didn't have the same advantages that they had."

That led to a key insight for Jim: "People tend to think that growing up underprivileged or in a minority environment is a weakness, a handicap. Ironically, in my case, it was the very thing that gave me strength. I would not, I don't believe, have been as successful. I define success as freedom. I don't define it as wealth or status and a collection of expensive toys."

People tend to think that growing up underprivileged or in a minority environment is a weakness, a handicap. In my case, it was the very thing that gave me strength.

His world broadened with an opportunity to go to Europe through a program that provided students a chance to study abroad. He says, "I ended up getting a full scholarship for a year at the University of London. I was a kid from a mostly white, very homogeneous society, living in a town of about 3,000 people called Millbury, Massachusetts." Jim says. "I didn't have exposure to other cultures. In London I encountered for the first time diversity of thought and diversity of culture. For example, my best friend in the school ended up being a Pakistani kid named Mushtaq Malik. I really didn't understand the cultural differences that set him apart from the Anglo students, but I shared a common bond. I, too, felt that I was being treated differently because I was a "Yankee" from America. I sounded funny. I was different from the rest of the kids. I didn't dress well. In many was, I, too, was a minority in that environment. I drew from my strength and experiences as a kid to say, 'You know, I've been different before and it wasn't that bad. In fact, I'm proud to be different.' I began to be proud of the fact that I was American and that I was different from the rest. You know what? It makes me more interesting."

This was the tipping point for his identity. As he puts it, "That sense of confidence turned me around. In the first six months,...I went around with my head down, feeling that I was being treated poorly. I realized that it was all in my head, and I picked that head up proudly and with confidence I created my own identity in this foreign country. All of a sudden, I became one of the more popular kids on campus and I ended up being elected to the position of 'head resident' of the student housing where I was living. My Pakistani roommate and I ended up being two of the more popular kids in the student community. It proved to me that I could handle any environment."

That experience helped him as he went on to become the president and CEO of 7-Eleven, Inc., the world's largest chain of convenience stores, where he worked for 21 years. As he says, "If I could go from being least popular to most popular in an environment that was truly diverse, with all kinds of cultures coming together, then I realized people are people anywhere in the world. That experience, ironically, gave me a tremendous amount of strength in going to Asia and dealing with yet another foreign environment that some people would have found intimidating or threatening. I embraced the cultural differences in Asia, which I believe contributed to the success that I was able to enjoy at 7-Eleven while managing a worldwide operation where we had franchisees from 120 different countries. That experience as a college student I think helped to contribute to success I enjoyed later in life," he says.

Amid his challenges as CEO of both 7-Eleven and Blockbuster, Jim had his "aha" moments in dealing with some of his transformational experiences. He says, "Once again, this is where identity is so important. When you become a public figure and you're attacked in the press, you realize this is just part of the territory. You must be able to say, with confidence, 'It's not about me.' The identity and the strength of character that you develop gives you the strength to be able to recognize that it really isn't personal. It's the nature of your role in certain organizations that you are going to draw fire, that you are going to draw criticism. You have to have the strength of conviction to know that it isn't personal. You must have confidence to know that if you are doing the right thing and staying true to your course, it will work itself out. The noise will diminish over time, and that negative momentum can turn into positive momentum just as quickly. The good thing about momentum is that it can go either way. If it seems like everything is going against you today, it can just as quickly turn the other direction with just as much strength and create positive momentum. A headwind can become a tailwind almost overnight. These are the things I learned in that senior role."

The lesson was that you've got to hang in there and be true to yourself. You've got to be authentic as possible based on what you know is right, and it's kind of stay the course. Shortly after Jim was first named CEO of 7-Eleven and took over in 2000, he had a powerful dream in which he was given three gifts that would change the course of his leadership.

The first gift was a willingness to change. The willingness to change is needed because "so often we [get] locked on a path, and yet the world changes every single day," Jim says. "Particularly in a leadership role, you must be able to use information to change course, if necessary, because the circumstances or the environment has changed. Most people and certainly most organizations have a fear of change and develop an institutional inertia that keeps them from being able to adapt to the changing world around them.

The willingness to change is needed because "so often we [get] locked on a path, and yet the world changes every single day."

The second gift was confidence. "It's one thing to change, but then do you have the confidence to stay that course? If you are in an airplane and find yourself in a storm looking at that radar screen saying, 'I've got to find a hole between these two thunderstorms,' do you have the confidence to stay that course and to fly safely through the storm? In the business world, it's the same kind of thing. Do you have the strength of conviction to stay the course or modify that course based on the best information you have?"

The third gift was the gift of simplicity. "We all encounter complications in everything we do," Jim says. "In the business world especially, you can't accomplish anything unless you are able to communicate and possess the ability to break very complex problems into simple solutions that are easy for everyone to understand and to follow. Simplicity in communications is a fundamental criterion for success in business or in life. I like to think of these three things as a roadmap for success in any leadership position, because the same gifts will work for other people."

> *There may be some storms along the way...but if they see those...as opportunities to grow and to learn, then their futures will be incredibly bright.*

Asked what he would say to young people today, based on what he has learned and experienced, Jim has this advice: "I believe that opportunity today has never been greater, but only for those who reach out and embrace it. That's the key. If young people today recognize that their identity is in their hands to create, to build, and that they can accomplish anything they want, then they have an incredibly exciting path in front of them. There may be storms or adversity along the way, but if they see those bumps in the road as opportunities to grow and to learn, then their futures will be incredibly bright. My most important message to young people, of any age, is that **education is freedom**.

I like this story a lot. Jim is a good friend, and I deeply admire the way he saw, at an early age, opportunity in his circumstances rather than defeat. In Uncle Lenny, Jim had one role model who made a difference for him. Uncle Lenny was the catalyst for Jim to make valuing a good education a part of his identity. To this day, Jim remembers Uncle Lenny's library, full of books. This inspired Jim because he equated books with education and his personal identity—and with his future success.

The difference between Allen and Jim isn't in their circumstances. It's in the way each of them viewed their circumstances. Allen just couldn't see opportunity. Jim could pretty much see nothing else. That led to a key insight for Jim. To quote from his story again, "People tend to think that growing up underprivileged or in a minority environment is a weakness, a handicap. Ironically, in my case, it was the very thing that gave me strength. I would not, I don't believe, have been as successful. I define success as freedom. I don't define it as wealth or status and a collection of expensive toys."

Jim had another very powerful insight: "I'm different. You know what? It makes me more interesting." These insights and the choices they offered up shaped Jim's set of core values in a profound way. And Jim lives his values. He walks his talk. Take some quiet time to complete the following values assessment process. Review the journey of your life. And in the spirit of the old Cherokee grandfather, consider which wolf will be the one you feed.

Values Assessment

How do you come up with your values? Look at the people you love in your life, think about what they value, and examine the times when you were successful in life and what made you happy. You'll find a common set of values.

The next page lists 75 values. What I'd like you to do, right now, is close your eyes and recall the people in your life you love to hang out with. List the top five (seven max). Write down their names, if this makes keeping track of them easier in the next steps. Now pick one of these people and ask yourself, "What are this person's values?" Look at the things this person likes to do, the things he or she likes to talk about, the kinds of television programs he or she watches, or the movies he or she sees. Is this person open minded? Does this person love to learn? Is this person committed to being good at doing something that matters to him or her? You get the idea here. Still thinking of this person, circle on the page or write on a piece of paper the seven values this person represents to you. (Feel free to add other values that aren't on the list.)

Now repeat the process for another person and do the same thing on your list. Keep going until you've completed the exercise for the top five people on your list.

Look at the page when you're done. You'll likely find the same values keep showing up. When we have people do this in a workshop setting, they usually end up with no more than ten values across their five people because of all the overlaps. Now ask yourself, "Whose values are these, really?" These are your values. It's that simple! Your values aren't your values unless you live them. These are the value you're living right now. And, yes, you can make changes. You can choose to keep different company to support all that is authentically you.

List of Possible Values

Achievement
Advancement
Adventure
Affection
Arts
Challenging problems
Change and variety
Close relationships
Community
Competence
Competition
Cooperation
Country
Creativity
Decisiveness
Democracy
Ecological awareness
Economic security
Effectiveness
Ethical practice
Excellence
Excitement
Expertise
Fame
Fast living
Fast-paced work
Financial gain
Freedom
Friendships
Growth
Family
Helping other people
Honesty
Independence
Influencing others
Inner harmony
Integrity
Intellectual status
Involvement
Job tranquility
Knowledge
Leadership
Location
Loving what you do
Loyalty
Meaningful work
Making money
Nature
Being with open and honest people
Order (stability, conformity)
Personal development
Physical challenge
Pleasure
Power and authority
Privacy
Public service
Purity
Quality
Quality relationships
Recognition and respect
Reputation
Responsibility/accountability
Security
Self-respect
Serenity
Sophistication
Stability
Status
Supervising others
Time freedom
Truth
Wealth
Wisdom
Working with others
Working alone

STEP # 2—CREATE YOUR VISION

You need to have dreams and aspirations that drive you, that follow the path of your values. You build your short-term and long-term goals from these. These encourage you to learn what you need to know, to acquire the tools for continual growth. They become the path to success and achievement. Without a vision and the goals and effort that drive you toward it, you are liable to flounder.

QUESTIONS TO CONSIDER

1. How is knowing and living your values essential to personal and professional success?

    ____

    ____

    ____

2. From our earliest moments, most of us are told to make something of ourselves. But chances are, the people who tell you what you should make of yourself have no good idea what to make of themselves. It's a mistake to make major choices about your career and your life based entirely on chasing a dream promoted by other people. Can you tell what's directing your life? Is it your values or those of others?

    ____

    ____

    ____

3. To be free, you have to listen to what matters to you, not what is blaring from the mouths of friends, foes, and family. What matters most to you?

4. How do you live your values in business and in the rest of your life?

5. Would you be willing to seek out new friends in business and in the rest of your life who talk and walk the values you aspire to?

6. Challenge your own vision and idea of success. Have you defined success for yourself, or are you blindly chasing some definition that's not really you? The enduringly successful people I know are all doing something they're passionate about.

7. Do you actually know how to get really good at doing something you love? Where could you find a coach or a mentor? Notice how folks on *American Idol* show dramatic growth with intense coaching and mentoring.

___

___

___

CHAPTER 4

Can Your Attitude Affect Identity?

I am a great believer in luck, and I find the harder I work, the more I have of it.
—Thomas Jefferson

When Rob knew Malika Sue Emerson in high school, she was always the person with ink smudges on her fingers and a notepad within easy reach. In English classes, she made the other students crazy by pleading for extra essay assignments. She wrote poetry and short stories, and she hinted to Rob that she'd started a novel but was a little young yet to have enough experience for the "big picture," whatever that was.

While the other kids were focused on football games, proms, and who was seen making eyes at whom, she strode the hallways loaded down with a backpack stuffed with books. For a while, she wore a beret, before being teased out of that. But she did grab at the opportunity on a nippy patch of winter to sport a long scarf that screamed artsy-fartsy.

It became the universal sport of her peers to pick on Malika, to mock her with bad limericks, and to avoid her company. None of that seemed to bother her. At the senior assembly, she read a poem that was so good, most of her peers thought she must have copied it from somewhere. But Rob had seen it slowly evolve during study halls and library visits.

One summer, Rob saw Malika at the Blakenfield town library. She had her backpack open on the table, and books spilled out of it. She tapped feverishly away at a laptop, her eyes fixed lasers.

Rob eased up to the table and let her see him before moving closer.

"How goes it in the literary world?" he asked. "Any successes?"

She slid a scrapbook out of her back and pushed it across the table toward him. Each page was filled with rejection slips. They covered a range of publications, from literary journals to *The New Yorker.*

"Why keep these? Doesn't this just discourage you?" Rob asked.

"Nope. It pushes me harder." She pointed to a pile of books about writing. Some were about sentences, others about syntax. She tapped a writing memoir written by Stephen King. "This mildly successful fellow says that if you want to write, you should read a lot and write a lot. I do that."

"Do all your friends and family support you in that?" Rob asked.

> *It's my decision to be who I am. If that's a wrinkle for them, they're the ones who need to adjust.*

She shrugged. "Some do. Some don't. The thing is, it's my decision to be who I am. If that's a wrinkle for them, they're the ones who need to adjust. One of the first things I learned is that to define characters well, I needed to show what each wants. What I want isn't big bucks or a name in lights, but to write as very well as I can and to keep improving on that. When I do that, long enough and well enough, the rest will all sort itself out until I have what I consider to be success."

Rob shook his head. "Well, good luck with that." He stood, and the tapping began again before he'd gone a couple steps.

"Now, that is one driven soul," he muttered to himself.

Five years later, he was reading the *Blakenfield Blast* online when he saw an article that Malika Sue Emerson would be signing books at the library for a charity event. Her second novel had been a breakaway bestselling success, and there was already talk of movie rights.

There was quite a crowd at the library, and Rob could barely make it to the table where a stack of her books was piled high and she was signing away. Many of the people buying the books were those who had once openly mocked Malika. One of them was the person in line just ahead of Rob. As Malika signed her copy, the young woman said, "Writing must just come easy to some people."

Malika's head snapped up, but she saw Rob standing there and lifting a hand to his face to suppress a laugh. Malika touched a finger to the side of her nose and winked at Rob. To the former classmate clutching the signed book, she said, "Yep, you betcha!"

STEP #3—DEVELOP YOUR TRAVEL PLAN

Whether you are starting out in the world or dusting yourself off after one of life's spills, you need a plan of action—clear steps you can take to achieve new goals. A clear plan allows you to focus on what's important to you, to stay focused, and to build or regain your confidence.

DISCUSSION

"The longer I live, the more I realize the impact of attitude on life. Attitude to me is more important than facts.... We cannot change our past...we cannot change the fact that people will act in a certain way. We cannot change the inevitable. The only thing we can do is play on the string we have, and that is our attitude. I am convinced that life is 10 percent what happens to me and 90 percent how I react to it. And so it is with you...we are in charge of our attitudes."
—Charles R. Swindoll

The big difference between Malika and some of her peers is that she made a clear decision of where she wanted to go and what it was going to take to get there. She had a vision, and a plan.

Malika...made a clear decision of where she wanted to go and what it was going to take to get there. She had a vision, and a plan.

What I like, too, is that she "got it" early and was able to sort through what mattered and identify who and what to ignore. She worked hard in repetitive exercises of her skill and made it work for her. Not everyone figures out their identity so early. Some are late bloomers. I'd put myself in that group—and there's no shame in it, as long as you eventually catch on and do something about it.

This is a true story. Only the names and locations have been changed to protect people's privacy. For a little comparison and contrast, let's take a look at another early starter, Ben Kaufman, who got his first self-starting business push when, at 14, he sat bored in a math class.

Profile in Success

Ben Kaufman, CEO of Quirky

Ben Kaufman went to Portledge High School in Long Island, New York. He learned in his own way, which didn't involve the completion of much assigned work. Ben had an idea for lanyard headphones, which he went on to pursue during his senior year. As he put it, while in a boring math class, "I was trying to listen to my iPod Shuffle without my teacher realizing that I wasn't listening to her. That was my first problem. The solution was a lanyard headphone that concealed the wires associated with the iPod Shuffle."

Those headphones, known as the Song Sling, became the initial product of Ben's first company, mophie (named after his two dogs, Molly and Sophie). The same day he graduated from high school, he officially launched mophie. He then attended Champlain College in Burlington, Vermont—but he lasted only a single semester. So Ben is a college drop-out, right? Well, that's one way to look at it, but it's not Ben's way. Nor is it the way of *Inc. Magazine,* which selected him as the #1 entrepreneur in the "30 under 30" category in 2007.

Ben, whose typical fashion statement is a black T-shirt, faded jeans, and Converse sneakers, seems pretty comfortable in his skin for someone his age—born in 1987, about the same time as the Internet. His parents believed in him, too—enough to mortgage their home to help him get his start. He started his first company at 14 years old. BKMEDIA was a web design/video production company with clients such as Maybelline, L'Oreal, Footlocker, and many more.

At Macworld in January 2006, he won the Best of Show honor for a modular case accessory system that he created for the iPod Nano. This allowed him to raise $1.5 million in venture money from Village Ventures to help push mophie forward.

Now, as far as identity goes, what kind of individual follows up on that by showing up at the next Macworld with nothing? At Macworld 2007, while all the other accessory companies were revealing their latest product lines, Ben and the mophie team had a booth made out of two-by-fours and unveiled no new product. Instead, they handed out scratch pads to 30,000 people at the trade show and asked the Macworld community to design the 2007 mophie product line themselves. Talk about confidence! On that day in January 2007, Ben committed to taking a product from sketch to ready-for-delivery in 72 hours.

Ben's "Aha" moment into his own identity came when he realized he wasn't so much interested in the end result as in the process. That was a key insight for him. He sold mophie and rolled all the assets into his next company, kluster, a powerful platform that allows its community to apply the collaborative brainpower of tens of thousands of people to collaborate on any problem and make a decision. Widely used by many major ad agencies, kluster is also used by various consumer product companies.

> *Ben's "Aha" moment into his own identity came when he realized he wasn't so much interested in the end result as in the process.*

The company was a success, but Ben wanted to transition back into product development. This time, he reached far beyond the iPod case. He formed his third company, quirky, a social product-development site built on kluster's collaborative decision-making platform. It brings the world in and lets product ideas become a reality, thus distributing the power of influence to tens of thousands of people. For centuries, it's been really, really hard for people who have great ideas to execute those ideas. They need access to capital. They need to know the right people. The people who are inherently designers usually find a way to get things made, but the people who are just great problem solvers are usually left by the wayside, and their ideas never get further than their own drawing boards.

Such ideas get submitted to the quirky web site at the rate of 100 ideas a day. The ideas come into quirky's product evaluation process, where the community scores and votes for them at the same time expert product designers and marketers consider the ideas. The resulting data is brought to Friday afternoon product-evaluation meetings, when Ben and his crew pick two they want to move forward with. From there, they go into a rapid collaboration process that includes everything from research, industrial design, and mechanical engineering to naming the product and picking colors, materials, and finishes—the things that move the idea into reality. It's the community's job to submit as many ideas and get as much data on the plate as possible, and help quirky sift though it all. When quirky puts a product on the web site, it basically says, "Here's the product. Here's how much it's going to cost. But we need to sell X number of these before we actually push it into manufacturing." In the case of a bendable power strip, Pivot Power, the brainchild of Jake Zien, the company had to sell 960 units before it could move on into production. Within a few hours of Jake's product launch, all the tech blogs were tweeting and retweeting about it. Jake was starting to sell several Pivot Powers per minute. The product made its numbers within a few hours, so quirky went ahead and moved it into manufacturing. Now, that's seeing the world of marketing and manufacturing with new and fresh eyes!

When asked by *Inc. Magazine* whether mophie will still be making iPod accessories a year from now, Ben answered, "God, I hope not!" And that's after quite a few successes with such products as headphone splitters, FM transmitters, and remote controls.

For Ben, the real key to his company's distinctive brand identity is the product development process, which can be summed up in three words: open source innovation. That's a popular way to go these days. Ben's the first to point out that the best products in the world are the result of problems people are experiencing. Jake's pivotable power strip represents that sort of product. Jake was annoyed that he couldn't fit all the power bricks into his power strip. His product and all the other quirky products so far represent simple problems that have resulted in brilliant solutions. As Ben admits, "Our products, at the end of the day, aren't all that quirky. They're real, good solutions to everyday problems. But the process is very quirky and unconventional. It's not what people would expect."

> *Open source innovation. That's a popular way to go these days...the best products in the world are the result of problems people are experiencing.*

So as long as there are problems, Ben and the quirky staff and its wide community will be there to address them. But knowing what I do about Ben, I imagine that his visionary identity will soon have him off on yet another successful quest.

QUESTIONS TO CONSIDER

1. What's your plan? Do you have an objective you'd like to achieve, a vision of your own sense of success?

   ____

   ____

   ____

2. Do you have a passion, a restless itch, or an insight for an opportunity that could be the mission or game changer in your life?

   ____

   ____

   ____

3. If you took a notepad and started to sketch out the action steps you need to take to achieve your dream, does it seem doable? Do you have the support of friends and faith in yourself to achieve your vision?

   ____

   ____

   ____

4. What training, practice, and effort will it take to get you where you want to go?

   ____

   ____

   ____

CHAPTER 5

Can People's Identity Change?

"The greatest mistake you can make in life is to be continually fearing you will make one."
—Elbert Hubbard

Rob started his first job as a clerk in a bookstore when he was still in high school. The thing Rob liked most about his job was his boss, Dutch Sullivan, a middle-aged family man in reasonable shape who was just beginning to lose his hair, which was turning gray anyway. Rob didn't know what to expect in his first job—maybe to get yelled at a lot and have to do all the hard work. But he quickly realized that Dutch was more like a father to him. Dutch read a lot, and he and the customers had many lively discussions about new voices and which books inspired, entertained, and enlightened them. Rob was always included in the talks, and that motivated him to broaden his own reading list. The exchanges also opened his mind to listening to different opinions and points of view. He and Dutch often stayed and talked long after the store closed. Rob found he could even confide the things that troubled him in his chats with Dutch, who never gave directives, but offered options to consider.

Tucked into a corner of the town square in Blakenfield, Dutch made sure the store acted as a virtual literary cornerstone of the community. He was a member of the library board, was active in a number of other improvement activities, and let groups meet in the store. The PTA mothers always had their bake sale by the front door, and Dutch never turned away anyone who had a reasonable request. Once when a young girl came in and looked at the same book three times in one week, Dutch realized she couldn't afford the book. Rob told him the girl, Kathleen, came from a poor family and had been ostracized by most of her classmates. That may have been because she hadn't been able or encouraged to bathe as often as the others when she was younger. But the stigma had stuck even though she had, all on her own, become the most fastidious student in their high school. Still, she remained an outcast, and poor, in a small town—never a good combination. The next time Kathleen came to the store, Dutch took the book off the shelf and handed it to her. "You can have this. A gift," he said. "If that makes you feel awkward, you can come sweep the front sidewalk some morning."

Kathleen clutched the book to her chest and hurried out the door. Rob watched her go and hoped that at some point in his life he would want something as much as that girl had wanted that book.

In the days ahead, Rob noticed when he came to the store early that the sidewalk in front was always swept immaculately clean. Neither he nor Dutch saw Kathleen doing it, but they had a pretty good idea who the elf was doing the chore, and it always made both of them smile.

Rob saw Dutch at the park, too, often playing tennis with his wife, Betsy, or playing doubles with their kids. When Rob told him how he admired Dutch's skill on the courts, Dutch gave him one of his old rackets and taught him the game. He worked with him until Rob became a formidable player in his own right.

Dutch was also a good mentor to Rob at the store. He encouraged Rob to read *The New York Times Book Review* and search the new titles for a fresh voice or an engaging read. He taught Rob the importance of knowing the tastes and interests of the people who shopped at the store. When Rob graduated and had the opportunity to head off to Champaign–Urbana for college, Dutch surprised him with a scholarship that he and several other neighboring merchants had put together for him. And Dutch said he was sorry he didn't have the money to provide all of the support on his own.

On every trip home from college, Rob would drop by the store and Dutch would pump him about all he'd learned and challenge him to defend his ideas in spirited chats. Each time, though, Rob noticed there were fewer books on the shelves. Where books had been crammed together, spines out, they were face out now and stretched across the shelves to give the illusion of stock.

"What's that about?" Rob asked.

"Times are tougher," Dutch said, sharing a forced grin. "But I'm still getting by."

Then one Christmas break, Rob came home to Blakenfield, and when he went to the store he found it locked. Brown paper lined the display windows, and a sign on the door said the space was available for rent.

Rob asked around and learned how the store had begun to falter, then failed, and finally gone under. Folks said Dutch could have blamed a number of things—the changing times, or a community that no longer shopped locally, or customers who shifted their loyalties to big-box chains. But he hadn't complained. He'd just quietly closed the door one day and sold the stock to a remainder company. Shortly after that, his wife, Betsy, had left him. His family had fallen apart. He'd dropped out of all the organizations and activities that had been part of his life. He was now alone.

Rob asked around, and his friends said if he wanted to find Dutch, all he had to do was watch the streets. They said all Dutch did these days was walk, haunting the sidewalks as he paced from one end of town to the other. They said he walked, and walked, and walked. Rob kept his eyes open and eventually saw Dutch's bent-over form taking long strides, his frowning face fixed on the snow-dusted sidewalk ahead of him. Rob hurried and stopped Dutch and almost reeled back at the weathered face that looked back at him. Dutch tried to smile, but couldn't quite manage it.

"Is there anything I can do?" Rob asked.

"Can you bring my wife back to me?" Dutch snapped.

Rob didn't know what to say to that, and while he was pondering, Dutch spun and was off at his brisk pace again, his shoulders bent like a brooding bird. Soon he was out of sight.

Rob wished he could have taken some action, but he'd been so stunned by the change in Dutch that he'd been speechless. He tried to track Dutch down, but his house had been sold and Rob didn't know where to look. He had to go back to school before he could do anything. While there, he gave Dutch's situation a lot of thought and resolved that he would do what he could when he was back in Blakenfield next. If he and the old gang didn't do something, Rob feared Dutch would be lost for good.

It was spring before Rob got back to town. The first thing he did was ask if anyone had seen Dutch.

"You'll find him at the tennis courts," said Sylvie Murphy, the owner of the appliance store that did business in the space next to what had been the bookstore.

That was a head-scratcher. But that's where Rob headed. He found Dutch, tennis racket in hand, and at least 15 children gathered around him. He was giving lessons. He was standing slightly straighter and, more important, he was smiling.

A cluster of parents sat in the bleachers watching, so Rob sat with them until the lesson was over. As he sat down, he could make out a new sign proudly displayed on the nearest fence that lined the courts: "The Dutch Sullivan Tennis Courts."

When the kids came screaming over to their parents, all excited and glowing with new budding skills, Rob went onto the courts where Dutch was gathering up loose tennis balls with a large square basket. He looked up at Rob and smiled. "You look surprised."

"I am."

"I'll bet you expected the worst."

"Well…." Rob hesitated. "What happened?"

"You're not going to believe it, but I was walking along one day—I'd been in a bit of a funk for a while there—and this young lady came up to me and said, 'Mr. Sullivan, can I get you to kick yourself in the butt, or do you want me to do it for you?'"

"How dare she?" Rob's face flushed and his fingers began to curl. "Who was it?"

"There, there," Dutch said. "Turns out that was just what I needed to hear. And you'll never guess from whom. It was that girl Kathleen who used to sweep the sidewalk for us. Turns out she's just wrapping up pre-med school, on a scholarship she earned with her grades, and is heading toward what I suspect is going to be a mighty fine doctor someday."

"What did she do that I couldn't have done?" Rob said.

"I appreciate your intentions, but I wasn't ready then." Dutch put the basket down and rested on the handles. His grin stayed in place, relaxing Rob. "I guess I still had a bit of moping to do. My back was up, and I was angry at the world right then. She talked me around that."

"What'd she say?" Rob asked.

"She asked me about the last time I'd been happiest in life, truly happy. I said it had been when playing tennis as a carefree young lad learning the game, excited about gaining a skill and feeling the zest of competition. She pumped me about my identity, too. She said I was a giver, a part of the community, involved, so what should I be doing about that?"

"And that led to this?" Rob asked.

> *She asked me about the last time I'd been happiest in life, truly happy.*

"Well, I had to practice, and people I knew saw me, and word got out. Someone hinted to the city council that teaching tennis to kids from all parts of town would be a good idea. Next thing I knew, the manager of city parks was twisting my arm and bending my ear. So here I am. Those kids who are just leaving are all from the poorer side of town, where Kathleen used to live herself."

"I like the sign." Rob nodded toward the one that now bore Dutch's name.

"Bunch of silliness, really. Damn thing embarrasses me." But when Dutch glanced toward it, a lot of pride showed past the grin, and he didn't look embarrassed at all.

STEP #4— MASTER THE RULES OF THE ROAD

You need guidelines to keep you on track—such characteristics as honesty, trust, hard work, determination, and a positive attitude.

DISCUSSION

Who we are never changes. Who we think we are does.
—Mary S. Almanac

In the true story of Dutch Sullivan, we can contemplate whether his identity changed. Did it evolve, or did it return to an earlier version? I think there are a couple of ways to look at this. One theory of identity holds that your identity is determined by the roles that you play out in your life. There is a whole body of writing that describes how social roles define your identity. At any moment in time in this model, your identity is a function of the role you are playing at that moment in time. Often you're likely to be playing multiple roles of varying degrees of importance to you. For example, you might be a parent, a teacher, a social worker, an executive, a friend, and so on. You probably find yourself changing focus and priorities as time goes by.

If we subscribe to a role-based model of identity, we could argue that Dutch Sullivan's identity did indeed change over the years; although at the end of the story, we find him playing out an identity rooted back to when he'd been "playing tennis as a carefree young lad learning the game, excited about gaining a skill and feeling the zest of competition." When I talk with enduringly successful people, they sometimes take on seemingly quite different roles throughout their lives. However, when I dig a little deeper, I find that changing roles are pretty much deepening expressions of a successful person's true identity.

This is probably a good time to revisit this idea of success. A lot of the time, the external world wants us to believe that success is all about impressive achievement, especially the attainment of fame, wealth, and power. Well, I've met more than my fair share of people who have fame, wealth, and power who are mostly miserable. Right now, you might be saying that you're good with the fame, wealth, and power thing—that you'll take your chances on being miserable. But it's not an either/or situation. The mainstream media stories about successful people, along with wishful thinking about instant gratification or a magic pill for success, may make it seem as if they were overnight successes, but it rarely happens that way.

People who enjoy lasting success mostly toil with every ounce of their energy and persistence, with heart and soul, for their whole lives.

People who enjoy lasting success mostly toil with every ounce of their energy and persistence, with heart and soul, for their whole lives.

They become lovers of an idea they've been passionate about for years, creating an obsession with every detail, losing track of time. In a real sense, it's something that they'd be willing to do for free, for its own sake. Quincy Jones wouldn't give up his music if it wasn't popular, nor would Nelson Mandela rest until apartheid was crushed. It's hard to retire from an obsession. Jack Welch is no more likely to stop teaching his brand of business than Oprah is likely to stop inspiring the human spirit. These people do something because it matters to them.

If your life becomes about building an authentic identity you express by becoming really good at doing something you love, and that something is highly rewarded by society, then you'll probably end up with fame, wealth, and power. But if you just go for the fame, wealth, and power, you'll likely end up being unsatisfied and miserable—and maybe prematurely dead.

In life, you're going to face changes. Sometimes you'll get the best of them, and other times, they may seem to get the best of you. How you deal with change in the long run depends on how anchored you are in the positives of your identity.

Remember, I said that your perceptions are often a battle between positives and negatives, and which side wins depends on you—on which wolf you feed.

How you deal with change in the long run depends on how anchored you are in the positives of your identity.

Let's pause to recall the first three steps of the process:

> **Step 1. Check your ID.** Find out who you really are. Success depends on self-awareness.
>
> **Step 2. Create your vision.** A well-defined vision allows you to make meaningful, realistic goals for your business or personal life.
>
> **Step 3. Develop a travel plan.** Create a plan of action that allows you to work toward your goals.

Now, you can extend from that by developing rules that keep you on track, focused on a purpose that promises you your version of success. Change may cause you to feel confused, out of sorts, and you need to focus on what makes you, well, you—your identity. You need to have rules in place. What positive qualities will help you? Such characteristics as honesty, trust, hard work, determination, and a positive attitude.

So when you have to stop and reboot, these rules kick in—maybe not at first, but when you need them most, if you do this right. They'll help you stabilize, adapt, and, if necessary, find the new you—or, at least, what you perceive is your identity.

You're going to make mistakes, and you're going to make choices—some bad. You're going to be handed the short end of the stick sometimes, even when you did nothing wrong. Dust yourself off. Get over it. And revisit your rules.

Your rules should be building around the core of your values and the aspects of you that aren't likely to change. If you're an introvert, it isn't likely that you can suddenly become an extrovert. Some things you can adjust. Earlier, I admitted I wasn't the thinker that Oprah is. But I did improve on that. There are things you can do in dealing with change. And if you've followed the process, you'll find a wholesome, healthy, ongoing you—rich in the identity of values—to help you reboot and get started again.

In the next section, you meet Steve Jobs, who embraced a number of roles and faced extraordinary challenges in his all-too-short lifetime. Ask yourself whether his identity changed or whether he took on a portfolio of roles in which he practiced the intense expression of his core values and identity. To be successful in any of the roles you take on in your life, you have to fill the role with the spirit of your real self, your passion, and your values. This is your true identity. It can become stronger over time as you learn and grow and stop attempting or pretending to be what you think the external world wants you to be. You might just find yourself saying to folks, "You know, I used to be different, but now I'm the same." They probably won't know what on earth you're talking about. But you will. You will know that you've

To be successful in any of the roles you take on in your life, you have to fill the role with the spirit of your real self, your passion, and your values.

stopped letting the world drop in the quarters and press your buttons so that you play their tune. You'll be playing your own tune, stepping into your greatness. You'll be comfortable in your own skin because the internal you and the external you will match. In spirit, they will be very much the same—not different anymore.

Profile in Success
Steve Jobs, late CEO of Apple Computer

Steve Jobs gave the following commencement address at Stanford University on June 12, 2005. Jobs died of pancreatic cancer in October 2011. There's no need for me to elaborate on his life and iconic legacy; his eloquent stories do that for me.

I am honored to be with you today at your commencement from one of the finest universities in the world. I never graduated from college. Truth be told, this is the closest I've ever gotten to a college graduation. Today I want to tell you three stories from my life. That's it. No big deal. Just three stories.

The first story is about connecting the dots.

I dropped out of Reed College after the first 6 months, but then stayed around as a drop-in for another 18 months or so before I really quit. So why did I drop out?

It started before I was born. My biological mother was a young, unwed college graduate student, and she decided to put me up for adoption. She felt very strongly that I should be adopted by college graduates, so everything was all set for me to be adopted at birth by a lawyer and his wife. Except that when I popped out, they decided at the last minute that they really wanted a girl. So my parents, who were on a waiting list, got a call in the middle of the night asking, "We have an unexpected baby boy; do you want him?" They said, "Of course." My biological mother later found out that my mother had never graduated from college and that my father had never graduated from high school. She refused to sign the final adoption papers. She only relented a few months later when my parents promised that I would someday go to college.

And 17 years later, I did go to college. But I naively chose a college that was almost as expensive as Stanford, and all of my working-class parents' savings were being spent on my college tuition. After six months, I couldn't see the value in it. I had no idea what I wanted to do with my life and no idea how college was going to help me figure it out. And here I was spending all of the money my parents had saved their entire life. So I decided to drop out and trust that it would all work out okay. It was pretty scary at the time, but looking back, it was one of the best decisions I ever made. The minute I dropped out, I could stop taking the required classes that didn't interest me and begin dropping in on the ones that looked interesting.

Much of what I stumbled into by following my curiosity and intuition turned out to be priceless later on.

It wasn't all romantic. I didn't have a dorm room, so I slept on the floor in friends' rooms, I returned Coke bottles for the 5¢ deposits to buy food with, and I would walk the seven miles across town every Sunday night to get one good meal a week at the Hare Krishna temple. I loved it. And much of what I stumbled into by following my curiosity and intuition turned out to be priceless later on. Let me give you one example:

Reed College at that time offered perhaps the best calligraphy instruction in the country. Throughout the campus, every poster, every label on every drawer, was beautifully hand calligraphed. Because I had dropped out and didn't have to take the normal classes, I decided to take a calligraphy class to learn how to do this. I learned about serif and san serif typefaces, about varying the amount of space between different letter combinations, about what makes great typography great. It was beautiful, historical, artistically subtle in a way that science can't capture, and I found it fascinating.

None of this had even a hope of any practical application in my life. But ten years later, when we were designing the first Macintosh computer, it all came back to me. And we designed it all into the Mac. It was the first computer with beautiful typography. If I had never dropped in on that single course in college, the Mac would have never had multiple typefaces or proportionally spaced fonts. And since Windows just copied the Mac, it's likely that no personal computer would have them. If I had never dropped out, I would have never dropped in on this calligraphy class, and personal computers might not have the wonderful typography that they do. Of course, it was impossible to connect the dots looking forward when I was in college. But it was very, very clear looking backward ten years later.

Again, you can't connect the dots looking forward; you can only connect them looking backward. So you have to trust that the dots will somehow connect in your future. You have to trust in something—your gut, destiny, life, karma, whatever. This approach has never let me down, and it

You have to trust in something—your gut, destiny, life, karma, whatever.

has made all the difference in my life.

My second story is about love and loss.

I was lucky—I found what I loved to do early in life. Woz and I started Apple in my parents' garage when I was 20. We worked hard, and in ten years, Apple had grown from just the two of us in a garage into a $2 billion company with over 4,000 employees. We had just released our finest creation—the Macintosh—a year earlier, and I had just turned 30. And then I got fired. How can you get fired from a company you started? Well, as Apple grew, we hired someone who I thought was very talented to run the company with me, and for the first year or so, things went well. But then our visions of the future began to diverge, and eventually we had a falling-out. When we did, our Board of Directors sided with him. So at 30, I was out. And very publicly out. What had been the focus of my entire adult life was gone, and it was devastating.

I really didn't know what to do for a few months. I felt that I had let the previous generation of entrepreneurs down—that I had dropped the baton as it was being passed to me. I met with David Packard and Bob Noyce and tried to apologize for screwing up so badly. I was a very public failure, and I even thought about running away from the Valley. But something slowly began to dawn on me—I still loved what I did. The turn of events at Apple had not changed that one bit. I had been rejected, but I was still in love. And so I decided to start over.

I didn't see it then, but it turned out that getting fired from Apple was the best thing that could have ever happened to me. The heaviness of being successful was replaced by the lightness of being a beginner again, less sure about everything. It freed me to enter one of the most creative periods of my life.

During the next five years, I started a company named NeXT, another company named Pixar, and fell in love with an amazing woman who would become my wife. Pixar went on to create the world's first computer-animated feature film, *Toy Story*, and is now the most successful animation studio in the world. In a remarkable turn of events, Apple bought NeXT, I returned to Apple, and the technology we developed at NeXT is at the heart of Apple's current renaissance. And Laurene and I have a wonderful family together.

I'm pretty sure none of this would have happened if I hadn't been fired from Apple. It was awful-tasting medicine, but I guess the patient needed it. Sometimes life hits you in the head with a brick. Don't lose faith. I'm convinced that the only thing that kept me going was that I loved what I did. You've got to find what you love. And that is as true for your work as it is for your lovers. Your work is going to

Sometimes life hits you in the head with a brick. Don't lose faith...the only thing that kept me going was that I loved what I did.

fill a large part of your life, and the only way to be truly satisfied is to do what you believe is great work. And the only way to do great work is to love what you do. If you haven't found it yet, keep looking. Don't settle. As with all matters of the heart, you'll know when you find it. And like any great relationship, it just gets better and better as the years roll on. So keep looking until you find it. Don't settle.

My third story is about death.

When I was 17, I read a quote that went something like, "If you live each day as if it was your last, someday you'll most certainly be right." It made an impression on me, and since then, for the past 33 years, I have looked in the mirror every morning and asked myself, "If today were the last day of my life, would I want to do what I am about to do today?" And whenever the answer has been "No" for too many days in a row, I know I need to change something.

Remembering that I'll be dead soon is the most important tool I've ever encountered to help me make the big choices in life. Because almost everything—all external expectations, all pride, all fear of embarrassment or failure—these things just fall away in the face of death, leaving only what is truly important. Remembering that you are going to die is the best way I know to avoid the trap of thinking you have something to lose. You are already naked. There is no reason not to follow your heart.

About a year ago, I was diagnosed with cancer. I had a scan at 7:30 in the morning, and it clearly showed a tumor on my pancreas. I didn't even know what a pancreas was.

The doctors told me this was almost certainly a type of cancer that is incurable, and that I should expect to live no longer than three to six months. My doctor advised me to go home and get my affairs in order, which is doctor's code for "Prepare to die." It means to try to tell your kids everything you thought you'd have the next ten years to tell them in just a few months. It means to make sure everything is buttoned up so that it will be as easy as possible for your family. It means to say your goodbyes.

I lived with that diagnosis all day. Later that evening, I had a biopsy, where they stuck an endoscope down my throat, through my stomach, and into my intestines; put a needle into my pancreas; and got a few cells from the tumor. I was sedated, but my wife, who was there, told me that when they viewed the cells under a microscope, the doctors started crying because it turned out to be a very rare form of pancreatic cancer that is curable with surgery. I had the surgery, and I'm fine now.

This was the closest I've been to facing death, and I hope it's the closest I get for a few more decades. Having lived through it, I can now say this to you with a bit more certainty than when death was a useful but purely intellectual concept:

No one wants to die. Even people who want to go to heaven don't want to die to get there. And yet death is the destination we all share. No one has ever escaped it. And that is as it should be, because Death is very likely the single best invention of Life. It is Life's change agent. It clears out the old to make way for the new. Right now the new is you, but someday not too long from now, you will gradually become the old and be cleared away. Sorry to be so dramatic, but it is quite true.

Your time is limited, so don't waste it living someone else's life. Don't be trapped by dogma—which is living with the results of other people's thinking. Don't let the noise of others' opinions drown out your own inner voice. And most important, have the courage to follow your heart and intuition. They somehow already know what you truly want to become. Everything else is secondary.

Don't let the noise of others' opinions drown out your own inner voice...have the courage to follow your heart and intuition.

When I was young, there was an amazing publication called *The Whole Earth Catalog*, which was one of the bibles of my generation. It was created by a fellow named Stewart Brand not far from here in Menlo Park, and he brought it to life with his poetic touch. This was in the late 1960s, before personal computers and desktop publishing, so it was all made with typewriters, scissors, and Polaroid cameras. It was sort of like Google in paperback form, 35 years before Google came along: It was idealistic and overflowing with neat tools and great notions.

Stewart and his team put out several issues of *The Whole Earth Catalog*, and then when it had run its course, they put out a final issue. It was the mid-1970s, and I was

> your age. On the back cover of their final issue was a photograph of an early morning country road, the kind you might find yourself hitchhiking on if you were so adventurous. Beneath it were the words "Stay Hungry. Stay Foolish." It was their farewell message as they signed off. Stay hungry. Stay foolish. And I have always wished that for myself. And now, as you graduate to begin anew, I wish that for you.
>
> Stay hungry. Stay foolish.
>
> Thank you all very much.

Every time I read this, I am deeply moved. In so may ways, it is an impossible story, starting with the fact that his biological mother did not have an abortion when she found herself pregnant with Steve. If you wrote this story as a work of fiction, critics would complain that it was too far removed from reality to be taken seriously. Yet true it is, and people who knew him will tell you there was no ambiguity about the identity called Steve Jobs. Here is a man whose passion for great design and exceptional user experiences has changed the way most of us interact with our world. I think Steve would be happy if we think of him as a champion of real identity because he invented so many ways for us to express ourselves as passionate and authentic individuals.

As he came to terms with his death arriving sooner than he hoped, he also came to terms with the idea that no one is indispensable. And then he worked until the day before his death, making Apple indispensable in our lives.

QUESTIONS TO CONSIDER

1. What are your core positive values that you think you can most rely upon when the going gets tough or the ground shifts out from under you?

 ____

 ____

 ____

2. What rules can you make for yourself? Would "Stay hungry" and "Stay foolish" be among them?

 ____

 ____

 ____

3. Who can you turn to for support? What relationships, affiliations, friends, and acquaintances can you count on when the going gets rough?

 ____

 ____

 ____

CHAPTER 6

Do You Transform Your Own Identity? Or Is It Owning Your Identity That Transforms Your Life?

Not everything that is faced can be changed.
But nothing can be changed until it is faced.
—James Baldwin

One of the things Rob liked most about his almost daily visits to Blakenfield's biggest city park wasn't just the chance to shoot hoops or play tennis with his friends, but to see people from all walks of the community coming together to enjoy the sun and the outdoors. Perhaps the most interesting person of all was a young woman named Tomika who often brought an easel and set it up by the swings and slides so she could paint while her two small kids, Sue Beth and Tomas, played.

The first time or two Rob saw her with her easel, he thought she must be a dabbler, a hobbiest who got a kick out of messing with paint. But when he got a good look at one of her works-in-progress, he could tell even then that her work was good—punch-you-in-the-stomach good. She had caught the sway of trees above the Frisbee golf course as the tops breathed and embraced the sky. Her painting came to life on the canvas, enough to move the viewer emotionally. Rob couldn't believe her skill and thought at first she must just be someone gifted. Then he watched her work and realized it was more like that old joke, "How do you get to Carnegie Hall? Practice."

Rob could imagine that Tomika had spent quite a few hours getting to her level of accomplishment.

One summer afternoon, though, she seemed to be in a more thoughtful state. Tomas screamed as he rocketed down the slide, and Sue Beth giggled from a swing, but Tomika held her palette and merely stared at the blank canvas on her easel. Her mind seemed far, far away.

Rob had finished up his basketball game with the guys and sat resting by the court. He thought he might go and ask her how she was doing, but her still, thoughtful intensity made him stay seated, drinking his Gatorade.

She suddenly exploded, kicking over the easel and knocking the canvas to the ground. Tomika tugged the palette off her hand and threw it down on top of the canvas. Then she screamed and kicked it again.

Rob jumped to his feet and rushed over, looking to see that the kids were still playing and hadn't seen their mother lose her cool. When Rob got close to Tomika, she spun. Her fists were clenched, and tears streamed down both cheeks. He thought for a second she was going to punch him. Instead, she stood there, with great wracking sobs shaking her whole body.

"What in the world is wrong?" Rob said. He knew she was a single mother. But that didn't seem likely to be what had made her snap. Her two kids still played happily.

"Oh, it's just work," she said. "It's stealing from me what I want to do: Create. That's what I'm really passionate about."

"Well," Rob said. "I guess anger is one passion."

When that just darkened her frown, he said, "How are they stealing from you?'

"I work for a printer. I was only supposed to be doing routine touch-up work, fixing things. When my boss found out I paint, he kind of loaned me out to a friend to work on a project that is going to be very profitable. But I'm doing the core of the work, the part that's going to make it work, and I'm getting paid squat. Worse, when I come home, I have nothing creative left in me. They're stealing my best juice. There's nothing for me, and I can't do anything about it. I need the job. I've got two kids, and they have no father. I'm 26. I'm half Asian and half Hispanic, with no real advanced education. Minimum-wage material. At least, that's how my boss sees me. It makes me so angry, but I can do so little about it. I feel trapped, like I'm a slave."

"Hmm, I don't know," Rob responded. "Aren't you always practicing at your painting, and isn't this just one more opportunity to hone your skills?"

"You don't understand," she replied. "This isn't what I was hired for. They're taking something from me—my creative juice. And the compensation isn't right or fair. It feels abusive to me."

The kids, Sue Beth and Tomas, had turned and were looking toward their mother. She waved to them. "It's okay. Go ahead and play. We're just talking."

"Maybe we'd better sit down," Rob said. "I want to talk to you about this."

"Okay." She lowered herself beside her toppled easel and started gathering up the palette and her brushes. "I come home, and I have nothing," she said. "I just wish I had options. But I don't."

Everyone has options. Sometimes the person doesn't know it.

"I don't know," Rob said. "Everyone has options. Sometimes the person doesn't know it. For instance, I heard you using a lot of labels, like you're pigeonholed into being just what your perception is of you now. There's a way around that, you know."

"Really?" She looked up, rubbing at one wet cheek. But for the first time, faint hope glittered in those dark eyes.

"The first thing you probably need to do is reject the labels others have pinned on you," Rob said. "You can come up with a whole lot more positive ways of looking at yourself than that. Aspiring artist, for instance—and a darned good one, I suspect."

"But how? It's useless to dream when it can never happen," Tomika said. "I'm trapped."

"That's one of the labels, Tomika, one of the negative ones. I think if you talk to the right people, you'll find you can shake those mental shackles as if they were cheap plastic."

"Really?"

"Look, I'll set up a meeting at Starbucks," Rob offered. "Let me know when you can make it, and I'll have some people you can talk to, who might show you that you really do have options. Okay?"

"Are you sure? You know what part of town I live in, don't you?"

"Another label, Tomika. One of the people I'm going to try to round up grew up within a block or two of where you live."

A week later, Rob looked up from his coffee to see Tomika come in the front door of the shop. Her hopeful smile was a good sign that she'd gotten some of the more positive parts of her passion back. Good for her, he thought. Good for her.

"I got my Mom to watch the kids. My, you've got quite a gang with you. Who are these people?" she asked Rob.

"This is my former boss, Dutch, who teaches tennis at the park. Sylvie runs a store here in town. Kathleen is a pre-med student who grew up right where you did. And this guy in the spiffy suit is Steve, from the bank."

"The bank?"

"I'll get her a coffee while you explain," Dutch said.

"I'm going to let Kathleen tell you," Rob said. "Because she fought her way past quite a few labels herself to head for her success. Take it away, Kathleen."

Kathleen leaned forward, her elbows and forearms on the table. "Let me ask you first of all if you still feel you're being ripped off. That you want to do something about giving all of what's most important to you to someone else who doesn't fully appreciate it."

"Yes," Tomika said. The word quivered and seemed to hang in the air. "My boss is nice enough, and so is his friend. But they don't get me, know how I feel, and I certainly don't think I'm getting paid what I deserve. I instead feel like a slave, one who's been sold down the river."

"And how would you define success?" Kathleen asked. "Is it just freedom from that, or more?"

"I'd just like to be able to make enough to be in control of my own life," Tomika said. "Then I could do what I want, paint in free time I've earned."

"Labels, labels, labels," Kathleen muttered. "Wrong side of town is one I battled, among others. You seem to know in pretty clear detail who and what you are. But you're going to have to work past the perception that other people are the ones holding you back, that they're in control of your life. You're in control—or, at least, can be. I think you and I are going to have to have a long talk about your vision, how to plan toward it. But first, you have to decide whether to leap or not to leap. There's risk in everything. But if you're focused on the reward, that you'll get to live your life on your terms, with all the creative time you want, and can claim your efforts for your own and be rewarded for them in the way you should be, then you're going to have to take a deep breath and say, 'Let's do this thing.' Are you ready for that?"

> *Work past the perception that other people are the ones holding you back, that they're in control of your life. You're in control—or, at least, can be.*

Tomika nodded, slowly at first, then with more vigor.

Sylvie brushed back a loose lock of curly red hair. Rob knew she probably dyed it, since she was in her seventies. She leaned closer. "Let me explain the role of this nicely dressed young man, Steve. He took time off from the bank with the promise of free coffee and a bear claw. Right, Steve?"

Steve was dabbing a crumb away from the corner of his mouth. He grinned and nodded.

"He's going to explain to you how a student loan works, honey." Sylvie patted Tomika's hand.

Tomika's eyes were wide, but in an eager way now. Her face swung to fix on Steve.

"It's just what it says it is," Steve said. "A loan so you can not only pay for tuition, books, and materials, but also have enough to take care of your family and get by while you get your schooling. The bank I work at believes that education for local people is the best investment in the future the community can make. You have to pay back the loan. But when you're making more money because of an education that opens that door to you, that's often easier than you think. When Kathleen here is a doctor, how hard do you think it's going to be for her to pay back the loan she took to supplement her scholarship?"

"I was just like you back then," Kathleen said. "I just wanted to get out of this town and start life over again, get a whole new identity. The thing is, I found that the things that matter in my identity were there all the time. My values. What I want. I just have to follow those like lights through the jungle. I've got to tell you, I'm feeling a whole lot better about myself these days."

> *I found that the things that matter in my identity were there all the time. My values. What I want.*

"You see," Rob said, "your perception is that you're being taken advantage of and are powerless to do anything about it. I don't know enough about your work situation to know whether that situation is really the case, but the silver lining is that it has motivated you to take action, if there is an action to take. You didn't think you had a choice. But you do."

"Look," Dutch chimed in, "this isn't a magic wand. It's not 'Pop,' now you're changed. This is something you have to want and something you have to do. People usually have to do this all on their own. But now you have an option, a place to start, and you know you have friends behind you who believe in you and support you. It's really all up to you now."

"I want to do this," Tomika said, her voice growing more confident. "I really, really do."

STEP #5—STEP INTO THE OUTER LIMITS

To grow you have to leave your comfort zone. Remember: Risk is a natural part of life; staying the same is standing still, and change (growth) means risk.

DISCUSSION

First comes thought; then organization of that thought, into ideas and plans; then transformation of those plans into reality. The beginning, as you will observe, is in your imagination.
—Napoleon Hill

When you see people adjusting their images, their exteriors, by costume, ink, or name change, you can bet they're seeking to alter their identity. But that's all superficial. Until they change what they value, they're just moving the furniture in their lives without making a real identity change. That leads to a more engaging question: Can you really transform your life? And if so, how?

The hardest part of any process for change is getting started, taking that leap of faith. Tomika, like most people, didn't realize she even had an option, a choice. But she still has to get started. With friends behind her and supporting her, that should be easier. But the final decision to leap is hers. In Tomika's case, it was a big leap. It could look like she transformed her identity, but to my way of thinking, she took a leap to claim her identity and take responsibility for her life. She resolved to stop casting herself in the role of a choiceless victim. And this is transformational in life terms. You may not be ready for a big leap, but that doesn't mean you can't take a step or two. What's important is starting out on the journey.

In physics, you learn that inertia is your enemy. If you don't know physics, you at least know it's hard to get up off the couch and jog, even when you know that's good for you. Same thing.

Transforming your life isn't easy. That's why having a support group of friends and family behind you can matter a great deal. And as Kathleen pointed out, when you change, you don't really have a different core identity. Your values are still there; you're just more aware of them and are acting on them. You feel in control of your life instead of feeling that others control it. It's certainly true that what matters to you can change over time—sometimes dramatically. As a result, you will seem to have acquired a number of new values, and if you live these new values and keep your existing core values, your identity will also have evolved. The operative word here is evolved rather than transformed. What looks like new values may be the recovery of values that were hidden away somewhere deep inside you, waiting to be owned. As I reflect on my own life and look at the lives of other people,

What matters to you can change over time...if you live these new values and keep your existing core values, your identity will also have evolved.

I see that as you become clearer about who you are and become grounded in your values and an identity that is authentically your own, your life will in fact transform (in a good way). The way I see it, identity evolves and then lives transform.

To get started and to stay in the groove, you'll probably need the help and support of family members and friends. Talk with them. Share your vision. Get them as excited about your success as you are. You might not even realize that there are other people who care about you and your success. As Tomika discovered, other people often do care more than you know. But whether you make any change or not is ultimately up to you. The ball is in your court. You have to make that leap first in your mind, and then you have to get started by taking action.

Once again, don't just take my word for it. Take a look at the life of someone who made something of her life and is keenly aware that understanding your identity is crucial to getting where you want to go. As you read Rosita's story, look for the themes of choice, evolution of identity, creation of value, and transformation of a life.

Profile in Success

Dr. Rosita Lopez, Associate Professor of Leadership and Educational Policy Studies at Northern Illinois State University

As a young Latina growing up in one of Chicago's poorest neighborhoods during the 1960s, my experiences with schools and teachers left me wondering whether anyone could succeed in this place of learning called elementary school. I grew up in a neighborhood where most of my friends spoke Polish, Ukrainian, or Spanish; an unusual few spoke only English. Initially, it felt like neither a rich nor a poor neighborhood—that is, until city street workers brought to my attention that it was just a poor and filthy slum. The news shocked me. It was an abrupt transition from a great feeling of being privileged to, for the first time, being "labeled." Until then, all I knew and cared about was that it was my home, with all the delight and innocence that only children can enjoy—blissfully playing games in multiple languages, trying each other's foods, and entering each other's homes with their distinct aromas and flavors.

Our parents interacted at the Spanish *bodegas,* fruit markets, Polish delis, and bakeries. Most of their interactions were gestures combined with the few badly pronounced words they knew in English; somehow, they managed to understand each other. For my parents, it was a triumph to converse with other ethnic groups in the community. They were proud of these interactions, and it seemed their survival away from their homeland depended on these brief collaborations. Eventually, with a smile and a handshake, they sealed their chats. Regardless of the language or culture, the adults looked out for us and were quick to reprimand us, followed by a report to our parents. They were also quick to pick us up if we fell and to keep us safe. The adults shared their specialties, be it roofing, auto repair, childcare, or other labor. It took years for me to understand that the sense of peace, comfort, and security was not in spite of our differences, but because of our mixture; we somehow fit in and felt cared for by this emerging and culturally diverse community.

Although my father worked in a factory, he was an avid reader and spoke seven languages. As a family, we believed that education was really important. I remember walking to the library and having my father ask me what I was reading. As the oldest of three sisters, my excitement about going to school for the first time was all I could talk about. My sisters couldn't wait for their turn to go to school. One of my favorite games was to role-play teacher with my sisters, who, without being aware of it, were also learning to read and write. I could already read many words in English, but the teachers didn't know that I could do the same in Spanish. They placed me in first grade instead of kindergarten.

That morning on the first day of school, my mother had fixed my long black hair into braids, tied with strips of colorful cloth at the ends, and had dressed me in one of her "native Puerto Rican" hand-sewn dresses. She was so proud. I tried not to let her down, but my tears flowed as she left the classroom. At the age of six, I was desperately trying to preserve my dignity by holding back the desire to scream, "Please come back…*por favor,* please…don't leave me here!" For days, I tried very hard to figure out elementary school, but I was determined to learn. When I wasn't sure about something, I remained quiet, observed, and studied the situation until I figured it out. Having been taught by my parents to be respectful, I spent too many days being quiet.

The majority of the people in the school, including the teachers, were Anglo-Saxon or Euro-American. I recognized a few friends from the neighborhood who had come from Poland and Ukraine, and, to my surprise, a few compatriots (a.k.a. Puerto Ricans). I knew this because we always stood out from the group—and still do. I sat near a fellow student who looked like one of my sisters and noticed that my friends who were not Latino started to shun me while at school. It soon became evident that certain taboo behaviors were not to be tolerated at school, such as chewing gum and intermingling with the darker-skinned students. At least we could still play after school and during the weekends, but to me, it never felt the same.

My parents had already taught me most of what I was being taught at school. Because of their involvement, I was regularly on the honor roll. It was apparent, however, that the teachers didn't have very high expectations for the darker students, those who sounded or spoke like me. They made it unequivocally clear that we were not their choice of students. ("Are you dumb? You must spic [speak] English!") A consistent message was repeated at every grade by enough teachers that it became intellectually dishonest to *not* get it. In the meantime, we learned other things, among them, the cruelty shown to those who were not like the majority, those considered the outsiders. We learned our place quickly or risked ridicule—or, worse, being sent to the principal's office to do nothing until it was time to go home.

Once I started to translate the teacher's instructions to a classmate who could not understand English, but midsentence, I was sent to the office for talking. It was hard to reconcile the rudeness of being interrupted midsentence. Upon these visits to the office bench, I don't remember ever seeing the principal. Occasionally, the school clerks assigned us small tasks while we waited, like filing and organizing or sending messages to classrooms. I became so good at it that the office clerks sent for me even when I wasn't in trouble. Sometimes I came home with numb fingertips from so much filing. I could spend hours away from the classroom in the office running errands or filing. No teacher ever sent for me to come back and learn the lesson of the day. It was disconcerting, even then, to realize that teachers, who appeared to be good people, could let this happen to their students.

I'm not quite sure at what point I decided I really wanted to do something different. At an early age, I knew that I wanted to be respected. I knew that I wasn't going to take this rejection thing, because I could feel people's rejection without knowing exactly why they were rejecting me. I developed this idea of real love to bring things back to the way they should be.

I remember developing a hobby of picking up little injured animals from the alleys and side streets of Chicago. Maybe a cat or dog that had been hit by a car and had a broken leg, or maybe a bird that had flown into a window. I had this thing about bringing these animals home, and I would take care of them until they got better, and then I would always let them go free. I've always understood that they never belonged to me and that when they were well again, they needed their freedom. My behavior puzzled my mother, although she embraced it without trying to figure it out. Later on, she told me that she figured out that caring for the animals saved me from being lost to the streets.

Looking around me, I saw that women had a different role than men. In the Latino community, this was very pronounced. The man was the head of the home, and the woman was supposed to be submissive to her husband. I understood this biblically because we grew up in a Baptist household, which is unusual for a Latino family. My father, all my father's brothers, and my grandfather grew up as Baptists. This also made us a little different.

Nevertheless, the message from society was, "You are a woman, and you are kind of lanky and brown, and you are poor, so you don't really matter all that much." I would look in the mirror and say to myself, "Oh, no, you are such a beautiful girl." I realize this was an unusual response, because I know so many beautiful women who look in the mirror and don't see their beauty at all. Perhaps it was because I was the eldest and I took care of my sisters when my mother wasn't around. I felt I had a job to do, and that was a beautiful thing. I took care of my sisters, and I also took care of the animals, so you can see that taking care of things is a core part of who I am and certainly a foundation of my identity.

My mother and my father were very positive with us. They never put us down. We were never told we were dumb, or anything like that. They felt that there was a beauty deep within each child of theirs. It was never about a physical beauty, the kind we could go out and flaunt. I always felt loved and respected by my mother and father, and I think that when you feel loved, you also feel beautiful. At least, I did. I also felt surrounded by love when we went to church. When I was outside this circle, I could see all the negativity, but while in my circle of my family, I was not subjected to the negativity.

Although my father spoke seven languages, including English, we always spoke Spanish at home. At school, of course, I spoke English. When I got home from school, if I continued to speak English, my parents wouldn't respond to me until I switched to Spanish. I realized later on that this was their way of letting us know that tradition matters. My parents never preached to us, but the lessons were always implied. In my case, this worked very well as

I started to assemble my own set of values and my own sense of identity.

Later, in the area where we lived, there were riots and killings. A strong sense that had developed within me from working with the animals moved me to protect myself and my sisters and the things that were important to us as a family. I remember having conversations with myself, telling myself that I could go this way or I could go that way, that it was always a choice and that choices have consequences. It got to the point in our neighborhood that if you made the wrong decision, you ended up dead. By this time, I knew that if you let anybody take advantage of you, which included introducing you to anything that was bad for you, then you ended up going down a path that could easily destroy you. I watched many people go down a path toward a darkness from which they could never turn back, because they got trapped. For me, it was about never getting trapped. Even today, I am very careful to make sure there is space around me so that I will not get trapped in a bad situation. I do this all the time when I'm driving. I make sure there's enough space around me so that I do not get caught in a trap that becomes an accident.

> *I talk to [students] about the dilemmas with which they struggle as they forge their own identity and work to establish their own qualities of leadership.*

When I talk with my students about identity, I often ask them to tell me about the parts of themselves that they reject. Of course, I also talk with them about parts of themselves they respect, what they're passionate about, and what inspires them. I talk to them about the dilemmas with which they struggle as they forge their own identity and work to establish their own qualities of leadership. I often find that people who come from poverty, who come from minorities, who wrestle with being different have developed the habit of rejecting themselves instead of rejecting the rejection that is coming toward them.

I caught myself doing that as a professor at the university in the presence of faculty members who were very uncomfortable with the idea of being a colleague of a Latino woman, who in their mind could have nothing to offer, based on gender and ethnicity. I remember that one of them said to me that I was there only because of affirmative action. My first thought was that he was just joking around, just kidding. Then I realized he wasn't. He actually meant it. I realized I had a choice. I could help him out of his bias and ignorance, or I could just get mad. I decided not to be mad. I chose to help him understand more about me and my background, what I had to offer the university, and the value I could bring to the students.

When you bring value to the world around you, you feel good about yourself—you feel successful.

Today our students must consider what they should reject and what value they can bring to the world. To my way of thinking, and certainly in my experience, when you bring value to the world around you, you feel good about yourself—you feel successful. I ask students, "What can you do that no one else can do quite the way you can?" We have open discussions, and I often ask them to write about this. I feel that when we privately write things down, we are more honest with ourselves, and what we value in ourselves develops a depth within us as a foundation of our greatness.

Too many of us tend to lose ourselves in our jobs and in how those in our environment treat us. If other people are telling us that we're really not important, that we're really not all that valuable, sooner or later, we inevitably start to believe it. I tell my students to choose carefully the environment in which they place themselves, because the choice has powerful consequences, for better or for worse.

This idea of finding your voice, of forming your identity, is really, really important. I remember that when I was around 15, I would offer my bilingual services to free clinics in the neighborhood. I would help doctors and nurses talk to patients who could not speak English, and this helped me recognize that I have something to offer—that I have value. So you can see that, for me, this commitment to providing value is, in itself, one of my core values and a key component of my identity.

I also love this idea of how important it is to love what you do and to do it really well. It seems to me, it's really important in life to learn how to get good at things. I went to work at a hospital. I started out by doing a lot of volunteer work, and then I eventually got a job in the hospital. I ended up working in the morgue, assisting in autopsies, and I became the best person at sewing up corpses, preparing them to go off to the funeral home. Can you imagine becoming really, really good at doing something like that? Anyhow, somewhere along the way, doing whatever was in front of me really well became a core value, and it has served me well.

My original classroom fear of becoming crushed and invisible drove me to the realization that I had to become recognized as a student of substance and potential. I had too much to lose and, for me, failure was not an option! Students should never be ignored as they sit quietly in the back of the room trying to figure this out on their own. Too many students spend too many days being quiet. Seeking tutoring, counselors, and extra-credit opportunities became my lifeline. It was here where *I learned not to be quiet anymore.*

QUESTIONS TO CONSIDER

1. Let's revisit the labels in your life. Which do you think are holding you back? How can you act on them, setting them to the side to head toward what you view as success?

____

____

____

2. Which of your friends and family do you think can and will support you as you seek to transform yourself? Have you left out anyone, like the people who surprised Tomika?

____

____

____

3. Challenge your own vision and idea of what success is to you. If it holds up to close scrutiny and is what you really, really want, what steps do you need to take to make this happen?

____

____

____

4. Are you ready to start?

____

____

____

CHAPTER 7

When Identity Must Deal with a Life Crisis

As human beings, our greatness lies not so much in being able to remake the world—that is the myth of the atomic age—as in being able to remake ourselves.
—Mohandas K. Gandhi

When someone knocked on his door, Rob answered, though he still wore his robe. There stood Dutch Sullivan.

"Come on in, Dutch. I was out playing basketball until they turned the park lights off on us at midnight. Sorry." He swept a hand across himself to apologize for being found in a robe at 9:30 a.m. on a Saturday.

"No worries," Dutch said. "I just stopped by to see if I could ask for your help."

"Sure. Help doing what?"

"You see, that's the kind of person you are," Dutch said. "You say 'sure' first and then ask what I need."

"Okay, what do you need?"

"I want you to help talk a friend down off a ledge," Dutch said.

"Really?" Rob asked "Is your friend suicidal?"

"He's at a low ebb in his life," Dutch said. "I know all the signs. I need to talk with him about pretty personal stuff, and that's never fun. It'd comfort me to have you along. Want to go?

"Sure. Let me get dressed."

They walked together down the sidewalk.

"Is it that close? I could have driven," Rob said.

"Walk won't hurt us," Dutch said. Rob recalled when Dutch had put in quite a few miles wearing out his shoes on these sidewalks.

"Where are we going?" Rob asked.

"Circus Bar."

"Really?" Rob glanced at his watch and shook his head. "I'm surprised it's not called the Dew Drop Inn. I thought there was some kind of law that every small to midsize town in America had to have one of those."

"There you go," Dutch said. "You have a good sense of humor. That's going to prove invaluable to you in life. Sometimes when you can laugh when you're tempted to cry, you end up feeling a whole lot better about everything."

They walked in silence for another block. Dutch finally said, "I'm glad you came back to Blakenfield to work a while before getting out to the rest of the world like so many of the kids from here do. Do you think you're a different person than the one who left here to go to college?"

"Well, the ones like Kathleen who leave to get a chance to be themselves somewhere else, I quite understand." he responded. "As for me, I think I'm more or less the same. But I understand myself better. I know more about what I can and can't do. I know more about what I want to do, what I consider success. I also know what I value. My friends and family are important to me. So I guess I'm the same guy, but with a richer, deeper understanding."

"It shows," Dutch said.

They came to the neon sign for the Circus Bar, turned off at this hour of the day, but with the front door wide open for business. Rob had never been inside and couldn't imagine doing so himself on his own, especially at this hour.

Inside, stale smoke hung in the air like bad dreams. A fake moose head with one antler missing stared at nothing from high on one wall. Most of the lighting came from signs advertising all the mainstream brands of beer—the kind that advertise at the Super Bowl—but this was sure no Super

Bowl. It was no Ringling Brothers sort of circus, either, and no Cirque du Soleil. Far cry from that.

The bartender looked up like Captain Ahab spotting Moby Dick, then frowned and lowered his head back to the newspaper crossword when Dutch pointed down to the end of the bar where one man sat with hunched shoulders over a half-empty long-neck beer bottle, with a smoldering cigarette in one hand. He looked up at their steps. His eyes were hollow burned holes in a blanket, with no recognition or enthusiasm at seeing them.

"I thought you gave up smoking, Clay," Dutch said.

"I gave up a lot of things," Clay rasped, his voice sounding like he was on his second pack of the day, early as it was.

"Let's move to one of the tables," Dutch suggested. Clay shrugged and brought his ashtray and beer.

When the bartender came over, Dutch ordered a Diet Coke and mineral water. He tipped more than he should have, and that only softened the bartender's frown. When they were alone again, Dutch leaned closer and said, "Clay, you told me earlier that the place where you work is downsizing, that you're likely to be unemployed soon. On top of that, your wife has filed for divorce. Have you done anything about that?"

"Done anything?" Clay's voice rose and showed the first spark of animation Rob had seen in him yet. "What the hell am I supposed to do? Life is dealing me the double-whammy. Am I supposed to just sit back and enjoy that?"

"Well, you know, Clay, there actually are some things you can do," Dutch said.

"I just wished I'd filed first," Clay said. "That's something I could have done. What are you talking about, Dutch?"

"There are two kinds of change, Clay. There are those forced upon you by changing circumstances, and those that you bring about yourself in order to create opportunities."

"What can I do? This crap has already happened to me. I don't understand even how or why. I can still remember when Clarissa meant everything to me. I knew I'd grown stale, tired of it, but I hadn't realized it was the same for her." Clay started to reach for his beer but changed his mind. He snuffed out his cigarette and leaned back in his chair. "Is there anything you can tell me to do that will make me feel better? I'm at the end of my rope here, I really am."

Rob was thinking that Dutch had been right. Here was a man who thought he was standing on a ledge in his life and looked just about ready to jump.

> *Whether change is planned or unplanned, there's always the opportunity for you to prepare for it.*

"Well, whether change is planned or unplanned, Clay, there's always the opportunity for you to prepare for it," Dutch said. "Now, I've been through a lot myself, so I'm not going to lie to you and say it's easy at this stage. But think of people in traffic accidents or natural disasters, or those who lose a son or daughter in war, or those who are crippled by war. Almost all of them didn't spend time preparing for the change that blindsided them. You're in a better position than some of them. You still have your health, if you quit this path." Dutch swept a hand past the beer and ashtray. "And you have friends, your values, maybe even some wants that could be rekindled."

"But what do I do?" Clay asked.

"Look, everyone has seasons of change in their life. They grow up. They get into relationships. They get out of relationships. They get jobs. Sometimes they get out of jobs. There are good times and some not so good."

Clay nodded. He couldn't manage a smile yet, but he and Dutch were sure on the same page.

"And we all get older," Dutch continued. "That's one we all know about and gradually prepare for. It's not like we look in the mirror one day and say, 'My gosh, where did my life go?'"

"I say that," Clay said. He lowered his head, rubbed his temples, and finally looked up.

"Look," he said, "you talk about planning for a change. That's all good and fine. But I'm already in one—make that two. I've been blindsided. What can *I* do?"

"If you're willing to work with me, I think I can help you build a new toolkit to help you through the process of change," Dutch said. "It contains some of the things everyone should have so they're better prepared for changes in their lives—and, believe you me, there *will* be changes. Some of the tools in this process kit are learning to control your anger, shifting your perspective so your focus is on the positives of any change, examining yourself to rediscover your inner good and your values, and developing your own rules that keep you on track as you face change. Look, I know you. Heck, I'm a lot like you, and I was sure knocked for a pretty good loop. I brought Rob along because he needs to know changes are going to come rolling toward him like some gripping scene from an Indiana Jones movie. There are seasons of change all through our lives. We all need to be better prepared for change. In your case, it's not too late. You've still got the rest of your life. You may not feel like elastic, but I'm betting you can bounce. Are you willing to work on this together, with your friends?"

Clay nodded. He blinked, as if waking from a long nap, a bad one.

"Well, what do you want to do first?" Dutch said.

"I think for one," Clay said, "we ought to get out of this place. It's starting to make me sick about myself."

"You've got it," Dutch said. "Come on, Rob. Let's go somewhere we can get a real breakfast."

STEP #6—PILOT THE SEASONS OF CHANGE

If you keep doing what you have always done, you will get the same results. Learn how to create change and manage your response. Dealing with changing circumstances is important, but creating and managing your response is even more important. You can feel stress when the pace of change exceeds your ability to change and events move faster than your understanding. However, with change comes opportunity and growth. So you need to prepare yourself better for change.

DISCUSSION

Einstein defined insanity as doing the same thing over and over and expecting different results. Everything I've been talking about so far represents a process intended to help you do things differently, to be ready to deal with change, no matter what. If you're alive, you're going to face change—and whether that's a death in the family or the loss of a favorite hair stylist or barber, you have to adjust.

The most important aspect of everything I've been sharing so far is that it is sustainable. It is like those natural resources that replenish themselves. So let's see how you can take all you've absorbed so far and use it to better prepare yourself either before or after a change. You need to

- **Check your ID.** Find out who you really are. Success depends on self-awareness.
- **Create your vision.** A well-defined vision allows you to make meaningful, realistic goals for your business or personal life.
- **Develop your travel plan.** Create a plan of action that allows you to work toward your goals.
- **Master the rules of the road.** These rules should embrace the people you care about and the principles that keep you on track.
- **Step into the outer limits.** Take the risks necessary to move forward in a positive way.

If you've been fortunate to have worked your way through at least these steps, you'll be better prepared for sudden change. But that's not to say a traumatic moment won't blindside you now and again. It's life, after all, and it doesn't always come with safety airbags and a roll bar.

What you most need is to be better prepared to pilot the seasons of change in your life—the sudden shifting gear ones as well as the dealing with a move, a relationship change, growing older, or anything that can rock your emotional boat.

The important point to remember—and it can be difficult to do so in trying times—is that life isn't always outside forces controlling you. At some point, you can get back in control of your life—and the sooner you do so, the better. That means

Life isn't always outside forces controlling you. At some point, you can get back in control of your life—and the sooner you do so, the better.

not doing what you've always done and expecting different results.

One of the really handy tools in getting your life back on track when it's been knocked off its rails is your ability to deal with anger. This has been one of the particular crosses I've had to bear, so I know everyone can get angry. Hopefully your anger is fleeting. But you don't want your anger to affect your judgment, your career, or your relationships. The effects can last forever.

Here are a few of the things you can do to deal with anger:

- **Step back and look at the big picture.** Think of long-term consequences. Can you get along without that job or without that person in your life?
- **Step away.** Go somewhere quiet to think. In a calmer environment, consider the effects of any actions. This could take a few minutes, or a few days.
- **Turn to positive action.** Direct that energy to active steps you can take. As in Tomika's story, you may find that you can leave a dysfunctional job for education that can better you. That's putting the "fun" in *dys-functional*. Or you might write resumes and search the marketplace. You may want to round up new

friends and build different relationships. You want to shake the negative and be positive.

- **Talk it out.** You have friends or family you can be open with about the way you feel. You may be surprised by how just sharing with someone else offers relief—and it also means that you aren't lashing out at the source of your anger until you're calmer and can speak reasonably.

- **Consider your options.** Dynamite is powerful because it's wrapped tight. Don't you be that way, too. The things that make you feel trapped and out of control may be getting in the way of seeing opportunities. Maybe this is a good time in your life to take that leap to a path that better moves you toward your success.

Life is also about seasons of change. Life has many. They're natural enough—like getting older, going out on your own for the first time, or being on your own again after a relationship crumbles. You can feel pretty much out of sorts, disoriented, sad, or lost if you aren't prepared.

These changes are as natural as the seasons in nature. Many you can plan for in advance, just as you know that, in fall, the leaves will change color. When you're prepared for planned changes, there's no reason for you not to flow better with the unplanned changes. Taking the steps to know yourself and the rules that reel you back to where you want to be can make all the difference in the world.

So far, we've looked at the stories of a few people who had to deal with some kind of life crisis. However, the intensity of a crisis is relative to the person who is living through it. And we cannot predict how we will act in a time of crisis until we actually experience one. Coming up next is a remarkable story of crisis, loss, and grace.

Profile in Success
Mariane Pearl

In February 2002, Daniel Pearl, the kidnapped South Asia Bureau Chief of the Wall Street Journal, *was beheaded by his Al-Qaeda captors. His widow, Mariane, wrote a memoir about his life,* A Mighty Heart, *that was adapted into a film. Here she talks about how her experience affected her own sense of identity.*

My identity was strange from the start. My mother is Cuban, my father is Dutch, and I grew up in France in an area that was very, very mixed. Mostly Arabic people lived there. Part of my family is white and part of my family is black. When I was little, in my family, the black people were poor and the white people were rich. And when I was very little, I also thought that everybody had the same circumstances—poor and rich relatives. When I met my first white poor person, I was very confused. I think my interest in this matter of identity started there, because I saw how subjective an identity really is. I also saw that people mostly inherit their identity. France is quite a racist country. A lot of my friends and the people I grew up with were from Arabic origins, and they went through a lot of acts of racism. Not necessarily overt, often hidden, but they were all obvious. I somehow escaped that, because I was from different origins, deemed exotic in France.

I am aware that I was lucky, for the ways in which my identity was different from others was not a source of pain for me, as it can often be for others. I also watched people around me suffer as they were torn between two or three cultures, and I escaped that, I think mostly because of my mother, who was a very inclusive person. In a way, I feel that the battle of race belongs to the past. Other people have sacrificed their lives to that. I felt I should move on. We are global already. Many of us today are a product of global citizenship. I am an American, and this was a choice I made. I think of myself as a global citizen, which is, ultimately, a state of mind.

I am always very uncomfortable with the public aspect of my life after Danny died. I am a journalist, and I told the story because it needed to be told. I did not do it because I was seeking fame. I am very shy about this whole social network thing. I have a Facebook account, but I never go in there. Real friendship takes so much to build. And I don't use Twitter. I just don't exist in this space because I don't like it and I don't feel I need to be there. It does not improve my identity; it does not make me feel stronger in my identity. I think I have remained unswayed by being exposed to the public eye.

The ground you stand on—all of your values and all your beliefs—well, that's your identity. For me, the way I dealt with all the anger, all of the frustration and the sadness, was by considering my values and discovering how strong they were. This was a very extreme case, when you have people in front of you who are determined, who are very clear in their message and very determined to carry on their war no matter what it takes and no matter how many people are hurt. When you are faced with people who have such a strong identity invested in their war, we all need a very strong identity to stand up to them. If you don't have a very strong identity, you get completely overwhelmed with fear and anger.

The way I dealt with all the anger, all of the frustration and the sadness, was by considering my values and discovering how strong they were.

The way I dealt with all of this was by assessing just how strong my values were. As I looked at my origins, at my choices in life, everything I experienced brought me to believe very, very strongly in human beings—well, perhaps not so much in human beings as in humanism. Humanism for me is a very difficult goal. It is a very courageous goal to be a humanist today. It accepts the idea that any change that is worthy today is going to have to come from inside of you, collectively from us. I found the determination to live that way even after what happened. And if I compare this to the terrorist's determination to destroy, mine is probably stronger.

My father was an intellectual. He was a very clever man, and I guess like so many people, he was looking for a way, a system that he could believe in. My father had a loss-of-identity problem. He was Jewish, although he didn't know that until later in life. It's a long and complicated story, and also a very painful story that I think is speaking through my identity. He explored various political systems, including communism, which is how we ended up in Cuba and how he got to marry my mother.

By the time I arrived in the world, people had fought a lot of these battles of the systems, and I didn't think it was worth it to fight them all over again. The battle my father led in trying to find a way to exist and find an identity to live within a structure, within a system, to me, had failed already. So for me, self-awareness and counting on myself was key. I realized if I was going to count on some system, on some government, for my success, it wasn't going to work. This was a big asset, because I didn't get lost.

I think the quest for identity never really stops. You have to accept this from the outset, because identity is always changing, always developing. For a child, no matter what the circumstances, the most important work is to identify the values that are the strongest for you. And you have to be very, very honest. Consider whether you are taking on that value because it's a good thing to do or because it awakens a passion within you. As a journalist, particularly among women, I have seen people do absolutely incredible things because they have been faced with injustice. Injustice very often brings forth from within us a strength that we didn't think we had. But because the greater good is somehow involved, it becomes fundamental to reach out to protect someone, to take that extra step to use all your energy and emotion. So identify the values that bring out the best in you and live by them. There are all kinds of

Identify the values that bring out the best in you and live by them.

lies and all kinds of difficulties, but the really sad thing is to leave this world without feeling that you have done your best to live up to your own expectations.

I don't know that there is one way to do this. In my case, my way seemed so chaotic. It has been an incredible journey that took me physically all places, emotionally all places, and it certainly has not been easy. What I can say is that there are a number of values. One of them is freedom, and if you ask me how I resisted hatred, my answer is that I loved freedom more than I did hatred. And this is the kind of choice you have to make, and it is going to be difficult to make the right choices—I'm convinced about that. The thing I would say to a child or young person is that this is a long journey to the achievement of an identity. Identity cannot be arrived at superficially, because it is never going to work. Finding your heart and who you are is going to be quite a journey.

I find a lot of things by reading. When I read—and sometimes I read very dramatic works—I find deep emotions aroused, and this helps me. I encounter ideas, and I notice whether they resonate deeply within me. I was on my own very early, and I was lacking direction. I wasn't being brought up in an environment that seemed obvious, because we were living in France but we were not French. So the way forward was not obvious. But on the other hand, what kind of person would I have become if my parents knew what I was going to do, what university I was going to attend, and on and on? I don't know, of course. In reality, I was left to find out all of this on my own. I accept that as part of my wealth today, actually. It is so important to be open and remain open, because the journey will take you all kinds of places and [give you] changes you never expect. We are much more complicated than we think we are, and the human soul is a very subtle mix of things.

You need a strong ground. You have to develop willpower, which is a limited resource, and you have to identify those stronger emotions that connect you with the rest of the world. To do this is a conscious decision, I think. This is the most important thing, because no matter what happens, when everything else has disappeared and gone, then you will know if your values are strong enough. That's when the trappings of success and all things that people run after are revealed to have no value whatsoever.

By keeping an open mind along the way, I have found out what really matters to me, and this defines my identity. What I thought I should be doing five years ago is very different from what I think I should be doing now or tomorrow. There is nothing rigid in the human life. You are always moving forward; when you're not, you're not even standing still—you're really going backward. This is what being alive is all about. New elements are always arising, and your ability to integrate them, think differently

You are always moving forward; when you're not, you're not even standing still—you're really going backward.

about yourself, and never let go of the vision and the values that you want to uphold is the most important part of being a human.

Throughout the darkest periods of the journey, I have managed to be loyal to life. In the presence of death, I've managed to choose life, and for this I am grateful. I think after Danny's death, in a strange sort of way, I chose life as a sort of revenge because I was very, very angry, and my first incentive was to oppose these people who had destroyed someone I loved deeply. I found in this the strength I needed to survive and defeat the anger and have the commitment to remain strong. I realized I was alone in this battle, and I could've succumbed to hatred—but then they would have won, and I couldn't allow that. It turns out that this aloneness is very precious, because it is here that you can find strength. Then you can go on and help other people find this.

QUESTIONS TO CONSIDER

1. Have you ever experienced a life crisis? How did you handle it? Is there anything you would do differently in hindsight?

2. How would you help someone else deal with the trauma of an accident, a death, a divorce, or a broken relationship? Does anything you've learned about identity so far come to mind as something that might help?

3. Do you handle anger well? What is the first thing you should do when you realize you are nearly "out of control" angry? What next?

4. How do you think you have weathered the seasons of change in your life? What changes do you see looming ahead?

CHAPTER 8

Friendship, Teamwork, and Your Identity

Lots of people want to ride with you in the limo,
but what you want is someone who will take the bus with you
when the limo breaks down.
—Oprah Winfrey

Rob heard the clatter of boards and metal tubing, followed by a yell. It was the yell that made him drop his hammer and go running around to the back of the house.

As he turned the corner, he saw a pile of 2×6 boards and metal tubes. Tangled in the middle of the mess, he saw Clay—or at least part of him. His head stuck out of the middle of the mess, and a bruise on his forehead was already starting to show.

Rob rushed to him and started to pull the boards away and toss them to one side.

"Are you hurt bad?"

"Well, I'm not hurt good," Clay said. He tried to grin but winced instead.

Rob was throwing pipes and boards to the side as fast as he could and had Clay just about uncovered when two women came out the back door from inside the charred house. He glanced up and saw Kathleen and Carol. "Just what I need," he said, "people with medical experience."

"I'm not hurt that bad," Clay said.

"He just doesn't want us to apply a tourniquet around his neck," Carol said.

She and Kathleen squatted and started to examine Clay. Two men came running around from one side, and one from the other.

"We've got him," Kathleen said. "You might try getting this scaffold back together."

Carol glanced toward Rob. "I thought you were studying engineering. Why didn't you help put this scaffold together?"

"I'm studying computer engineering," Rob said. "Kinda different."

Sylvia Murphy, their appliance store pal, stuck her head out the back door. "My two guys are just bringing in the new stove. They know how to put up scaffolding. I'll send them out here next. You gals did a good job with the painting. You could never tell the fire started in the kitchen."

"Who are you here with?" Kathleen asked Rob.

"These guys," Rob waved to the other guys who had gotten the rest of the wood and piping off Clay. "They're from the Kiwanis Club and said I could pitch in, too. Dutch was here as well, but he had to head off to give tennis lessons. How about you?"

"I came with some of the Junior Achievement gang," Kathleen said. "Carol came with me."

"Junior Achievement? I thought they were all about getting starts in business experience," Rob said.

"Putting a house back together where a family has been displaced by a fire is an achievement," Kathleen said. "What's wrong with your thumb?"

"I'm about as good with a hammer as Clay was in putting together scaffolding," Rob responded.

"Oh, my Lord." Melba Johnson stuck her head out the back door. "I hope no one was hurt."

"I'm fine," Clay said. "Well, not fine. But I'll be back to work in a minute. We're gonna have your house back together before your kids are even home from school."

"I can't tell you how much I appreciate all this," Melba said. "I had no insurance. Nothin.'"

"It's what communities do," Kathleen said. "Just like back in the day when a barn needed to be raised. We don't have any barns, so we're glad to help you fix your house. That fire was a sudden thing. But it looks like you have a new stove now, too."

Kathleen came out the front door later that afternoon as Rob came around from the back of the house. Rob held up his taped thumb. "Thanks for the first aid. Glad to give you and Carol a chance to practice craft."

Kathleen had a smear of paint on one ear and another patch on the back of one elbow. Rob thought she'd never looked prettier.

"House looks good, though. You have to admit." She glanced back and took in the result of everyone's effort.

"We may not be perfect," Rob said, "but we all got there in the end. The power's in numbers. Did you see Melba? She tried to thank us, but the tears of joy got in the way. I thought she was going to break one of my ribs hugging me, and Clay actually squealed before she remembered he'd been in a tumble earlier."

"I like it when things come together." Kathleen started to walk away.

Rob walked beside her.

"Where are you going?" she said.

"To the park. I promised Dutch I'd watch a bit of the afternoon lessons group and help him tidy up when the kids take off like so many speckled birds."

"Well, one of the speckled birds is my niece," Kathleen said. "I'm headed that way, too. I guess we can walk together."

Rob waited until she looked away before he let his grin show.

"I'm surprised you came back to town," she said after a few more steps.

I find it's good for me to be around people who have the same values as me. We feed on each other.

"I'm working on the people I want to be around," he said. "I met some nice friends at school. But I find it's good for me to be around people who have the same values as me. We feed on each other."

"How so?" She looked up at him with one eye narrowed.

"Well, it's like when I play basketball in the park," he answered. "Sometimes my pals and I aren't really as good as the other team, but we win. You know how?"

"I sense I'm supposed to say 'How?'" she said.

"We know each other well enough to flow. We give up the rock. We back each other up, offer a pick or way out, if needed. It's just like knowing someone's values. Trust is what oils the machine."

"I see. I didn't know machines bang themselves on the thumb," she teased.

When they got to the tennis courts, the lights were just staring to flicker on. The kids were running and squealing with all the hysteria and joy of youth. Dutch stood in the middle, directing and coaching. He'd sure found his niche.

The sky was just beginning to mottle purple and pink on the far horizon. Birds spoke with the softening clamor of settling into evening. Leaves rustled, as they are prone to do.

Kathleen and Rob stood just up the hill under a huge beech tree Rob figured had to have been there before the Pilgrims landed. A slight breeze came up the hill. It was a good time of day. They both seemed to be content to stand there and watch the children play while their parents chattered together on the bleachers.

"Why'd you come back to town for the summer?" Rob asked.

"You think that would be hard for me?" When he didn't answer, she said, "I had a lot to prove to myself and to others, but mostly to myself. I honor the things in me I think I see in you, Rob. They're good things—loyalty, generosity, compassion, and genuine love for your fellow beings."

"Um…well…um…."

"Yes?"

"Do you think if I asked you out, you'd have dinner with me?"

She looked up at him. "What do you think we've been talking about? Of course I would."

He looked down at her, at the paint on her ear and her bright, sparkling eyes. He leaned closer.

And they kissed.

STEP # 7—BUILD YOUR DREAM TEAM

Build supportive relationships with mentors and peers who can help you toward your goals.

DISCUSSION

This story is clearly about people coming together as an informal team to help a friend in need. Our protagonist, Rob, is very consistent about being a good friend, which is clearly a core value and a foundational character trait embodied in his identity. Rob also has a knack for assembling small informal "teams" to bring out the best in people. This is a core trait of enduringly successful people. They believe that very little that matters can be accomplished alone. If you have a dream, you need a team.

They believe that very little that matters can be accomplished alone. If you have a dream, you need a team.

I've learned over the years that people who create success that lasts have this idea that many of the people they meet are a potential member of their community or team—a recruit, a customer, a vendor, a volunteer, a friend, you name it. Here's where I'm going with this: Would your behavior in working with others change if you knew in advance that your relationships would last for the rest of your life, for better or for worse? How would you build relationships if everyone you worked with, bought from, or served would always be your neighbor—or, at least, the smart, talented people you wanted to keep around?

You can't hide in this global virtual world we all live in. You'll likely run into the same folks, whether you've intended for the relationship to be short or lasting, good or bad. Embracing this reality can be life changing, as you think about everyone as a potential long-term member of your dream team.

If you want a life filled with lasting success, you're better off thinking about your relationships as being built to last with people whose role in your life will probably change—sometimes they'll work for you; sometimes you'll work for them; and still other times they'll leave your organization and become your customers, your vendors, your regulators, or your competitors—and some of them will be your lifelong friends. But if you consider them all members of your virtual "team," the only thing that changes over time is their role in your life. You still have the relationship. And when you get to the place where you view your relationships as lasting, you'll behave in ways that respect and honor your relationships. You will be loyal to the best in yourself and others.

In your personal life, the difference between family and friends is that you can pick your friends. Some people act like their lives are a matter of circumstance and serendipity—whoever they meet has a good chance of being a part of the rest of their lives. Not so. At least that's not always the best idea if you want to be in control of your identity and life. There are fools and scumbags out there, and the only thing worse than making a mistake is sticking with it because you felt it was fated.

Now, I'm not saying that you need to take the romance out of love. I believe that the spirituality of love is one of the strongest and best forces in the world. Nor am I saying you should look for a companion by using a slide rule or questionnaire. What I am saying is that if the values of another person are what attract you to that person, you both stand a much better chance of helping each other achieve success in life. And I think you stand a better chance of having a longer-lasting, healthier relationship.

So it was with Rob and Kathleen, two thinking young people who may not land on immediate answers, but who carefully consider and ask, which gives them a much better chance of getting along than people who just fall together, as if life is a game of chance. That doesn't make them plotting, manipulative people. It just means they have examined themselves carefully and now examine those around them on the same terms.

Imagine that you walk into a room and are attracted to someone. Well, right away, attraction isn't understanding. You've had to take a while to get to know yourself, if you've been following along, and it will take you a while to understand someone else's identity.

Just consider those you know—yourself included, perhaps—who were swept away by a momentary attraction to someone based on how they looked, or their mood, or one beverage too many. I mean, if you're in the mood to tick off your parents by seeking out a "bad boy" or "bad girl," you may be the one paying for it down the road with quite a bit of sadness, in addition to being sidetracked from heading toward personal success.

That's also why staying fixed on your own vision or dream and, of course, your values matters. You need people around you to whom those values also matter.

That leads us to the number one myth about how to have a successful life: Just to have a dream is enough. It will happen. Really?

You're going to have to work and plan, and you're almost certainly going to need some help along the way. Success isn't a lottery, a matter of luck, something that lands on some people and not others. Success is a product of effort. The people with whom you connect as you strive toward your success can help you, or they can get in your way.

Success is a product of effort. The people with whom you connect as you strive toward your success can help you, or they can get in your way.

Now, think about this: What is the one thing you wish someone had told you about yourself, about how to know yourself and your identity, when you were, say, 15? Do you wish they'd said to be more careful in picking your friends and your significant other? Would you have listened? You'll face adjustments down the road. Consider Rob's friend Allen, who might have had admirable values and principles once but is now locked up for not paying child support and seems to be able to focus only on self-pity and a somewhat tangled view that the world has it in for him. Remember, you don't have to see the world as having control over you. You don't have to be a victim. And close friends who think that way aren't really going to be there to help you toward your dream, because they're stuck floundering in the puddle that their life has become in their eyes.

Let's look at some of the traits you might look for in friends, either the ones you haven't met or the ones you think you already have.

The Qualities of a Good Friend or Companion

- Are they trustworthy? Do they do what they say they're going to do? Are they honest? Open?
- Are they nonjudgmental? Do they listen without interruption and wait until they have all the details of a situation before they respond?
- Are they there when you need them? Think of all the people who responded when Melba Johnson's home burned. They did one of the most important acts of real friendship: They showed up.

- Are they honest and responsible? Do they pay their bills? Meet their responsibilities? Think again of Rob's friend Allen. No poster boy for doing things with integrity.

- Are they honorable, even in the face of criticism, temptation, or challenges?

- Do they tell the truth about themselves and others? Could you believe a resume they crafted?

- Can you trust them to keep your secrets? This isn't what happens in Vegas, stays in Vegas. It's the basic confidence that they're always considering what's best for you.

- Does their strength add to yours? Are you a stronger and more capable team member because of them?

- Do they acknowledge their own weaknesses and mistakes?

- Do they put the welfare of others before their own? Love, honor, compassion, and sacrifice are among the noblest traits you'll find in mankind. Seek them out among those around you.

QUESTIONS TO CONSIDER

1. Have you always made wise decisions when making friends, when dating, or with the people you most associate with? Do you wish you could do anything differently, or do over?

____

____

____

2. How have shared values played a part with you and your best friends?

____

____

____

3. Can you think of organizations in which many of the people share the same values as you?

____

____

____

4. If you had to start from scratch in finding someone for a friendship or relationship, where would you start? Why?

____

____

____

CHAPTER 9

Persistence and Your Identity

Nothing in this world can take the place of persistence. Talent will not; nothing is more common than unsuccessful people with talent. Genius will not; unrewarded genius is almost a proverb. Education will not; the world is full of educated failures. Persistence and determination alone are omnipotent.
—Calvin Coolidge

As I look back over my own life, and as I think about the great lives of the remarkable men and woman I have been blessed to know, I've come to think of all of us as works of art in progress. And the thing I've learned about great artists is that they hang in there through thick and thin. They don't give up. They're loyal to their values and their vision. Persistence has gotten to be a habit with them.

As you read Jake's story, consider an upgrade to your PQ (persistence quotient).

Profile in Success

Jake Steinfeld

Heard of "Body by Jake"? That's the tagline of fitness guru Jake Steinfeld, who has whipped many a body into shape, including that of Harrison Ford. Jake has also acted on the large and small screen and been the voice of animated characters. Now in his 50s and still one of the fittest people in America, here's what he has to say.

I was a fat kid with a stutter when I started growing up. My response to confidence and self-esteem issues was to eat lots of Twinkies. Also, I was brought up in a Jewish home where I had to finish everything on my plate, because if I didn't, Mom would look at me like, "What? It wasn't good?" So I got heavy.

Stuttering was a bigger problem. I was such a terrible stutterer that I was lucky I wasn't put into Room 222, which was for the kids who were called "special" because they had learning problems. Still, it was very challenging for me as a kid growing up. I could not get up in front of the class and speak. I couldn't even order a pizza, if you can believe that.

I tried the most desperate things while growing up. In class, when the teacher said, "Okay, everybody, we're going to read out loud. We're going to take a paragraph. Everyone take a paragraph, and we'll start." I would try to count the paragraphs leading up to when I had to read. So, I would try to memorize them. Now, it wasn't like I couldn't read. I wasn't a moron, right? But my stutter was debilitating.

All through my life, the stutter was tough. People made fun of me. Do people really understand? I mean, look, you don't make fun of cancer. But people laugh at a guy with the stutter. It can be a real stumbling block when you can't communicate. It was very challenging. But I'm talking now, right? My life is about communicating. The kids I grew up with look at me now and say, "Man, we never thought that you'd amount to anything."

What started to turn my life around was when my dad bought me a set of weights when I was 14 years old. It changed my life. Not only did the weights build my body, but more importantly, working out built my confidence and self-esteem, which I think everyone can understand. If you believe in yourself, it's amazing what you can accomplish.

My parents believed in me, too, and supported me, encouraged me. Most importantly, it was my grandma who really believed in me. She was the coolest. She took me to places I would have never seen. She took me to a racetrack. She took me to the old Madison Square Garden, where I saw Joe Frazier fight. As a little kid, she exposed me to Broadway, helped me see and understand plays. She did

> *You've got to have mentors you hang out with who are winners, and someone who buys into your plan so you can be a winner.*

all these different things and always told me, "Hey, you can be whatever you want in your life." I'm a big believer that you've got to have people. You've got to have mentors you hang out with who are winners, and someone who buys into your plan so you can be a winner. She was the one who mentally pushed me, but she talked straight to me, too, since I am the oldest of four.

I'm a big believer that life is about moments. My mom always said that I was the greatest. She'd say, "My oldest son, you can do whatever you want." So I decided in eighth grade that I was going to try out for the basketball team. I didn't practice much, but I loved basketball. I was a big fan of the Knicks, and I tried out for the school basketball team with a bunch of my buddies. After tryouts that Friday, the coach put a list on the gym wall of the names of the guys who made the team. I went with a couple of pals. I looked down the list, and my name wasn't there. I thought, "Oh, no. This coach is kidding me. Come on." I even looked behind the list, thinking someone was pulling a prank. But the fact was, I got cut. It was the first time in my life for that.

Then I thought, "Wait a second. I put myself out there. I'm not in my backyard. I'm not out with my cousins. I put myself out there to be with a real team, and I got cut." I'm telling you, it was a devastating moment. But I had a poem given to me by a girl in eighth grade called "Don't Quit," and she signed it on the back. It's an anonymous poem, but it inspired me and inspires me today every day:

When things go wrong, as they sometimes will,
When the road you're trudging seems all uphill,
When the funds are low and the debts are high,
And you want to smile, but you have to sigh,
When care is pressing you down a bit,
Rest, if you must, but don't you quit.
Life is queer with its twists and turns,
As every one of us sometimes learns,
And many a failure turns about,
When he might have won had he stuck it out;
Don't give up though the pace seems slow—
You may succeed with another blow.
Often the goal is nearer than
It seems to a faint and faltering man;
Often the struggler has given up,
When he might have captured the victor's cup,
And he learned too late when the night slipped down
How close he was to the golden crown.
Success is failure turned inside out—
The silver tint of the clouds of doubt,
And you never can tell how close you are,
It may be near when it seems so far.
So stick to the fight when you're hardest hit—
It's when things seem worst that you must not quit.

What motivated me was that poem and my dad taking the trains off my train set so we could use the cardboard bottom as a backboard. We had a little backyard. We got a hoop and put it in the backyard, and I shot all summer. I'm a lefty, but on the left side of the hoop, we had an overhang from the house, so I couldn't shoot from the left side. I had to practice my corner shot from the right side. In ninth grade, I made the team. Our first game was against Shreveport, our archrivals. You've got to picture me, okay? In ninth grade. I was 14, with an afro and braces. It was a great look. I was at the far edge of the bench, the 11th man. Our two starters, true story, collided with each other with about 17 seconds left in the game. They literally smashed into each other and got taken out of the game. We were down by one point. My coach, Mr. Cohen, looked down the bench and said, "Steinfeld, get over here." He told me, "All right, get in the game. Don't touch the ball. Don't touch the ball." I said, "Okay, coach." He was petrified. We had taken the ball out at the opposite end. I stood at midcourt, figuring that no one was going to pass me the ball, that they would go to Mike Miller, who was the star of our team, right? But everyone else was covered. They threw the ball to me. The clock was ticking down. I dribbled. They fouled me, with no time on the clock. It was a one-on-one situation—against Shreveport, our archrivals. Here I was, the 11th man, who hadn't even made the team the year before.

Shreveport was tough. They were all tough guys, right? They were all ninth graders, and I went to the foul line. I used to shoot a foul shot the way Rick Barry did in the old ABA, as an underhand foul shot. The ref blew the whistle and passed the ball to me, and I flipped it up—swish. I'd tied the game at 36–36. The other team called a timeout. I went to the sideline, and Mr. Cohen practically slapped me in the face. But I went back out there, swished the second shot, and I won the game. That was the kind of moment when I said to myself, "Man, I can do this. I can compete." I became the captain of the team all through high school, because Mr. Cohen went from the junior high coach to the high school coach.

I got my work ethic from my grandma, who worked every day. She worked at a hotel called Manhattan Beach Hotel in Brighton Beach in Brooklyn. And I got it from my dad, who worked seven days a week. My dad got up in the morning, put on a suit and tie, and went to work every day, Saturday through sometimes Sunday, selling. We were a middle-class family. That's what they do to get by.

I really woke up when I got to college, Courtland State University. I got into college because I played lacrosse. I wasn't that great, but they took me. School was not my deal. I just got into bodybuilding. I really loved working out. When my dad got me the set of weights at 14, things started to come together. Girls started to recognize me. I was no longer the fat funny guy, Jake. Now the girls would say, "Ooh, can I feel your muscles?" I was starting to feel good about myself. I was in college. I was doing it for my mom, right? I thought I had to be in college because that's what you're supposed to do. We lived in a neighborhood, Baldwin, made up of Italians, Jews, Catholics—it was all one. There were a lot of black kids in the neighborhood, but it was predominantly white. In our neighborhood, it was, "Yo, where is your son going to college?" "Oh, he's going to Harvard. He's going to Yale. He's going to West Point." But I wasn't at any of those places. I was at Courtland State.

I was there three months, playing with the lacrosse team. We were scrimmaging at Syracuse in 1977. I played on the fourth midfield, and these days my pro lacrosse players tell me, "Gee, Jake, I thought there were only three midfields at Courtland." So you can see where I stood. I was a face-off guy. I'd come on the field, face off, and then get off the field. Well, that one day in Syracuse in November, it was frigid. There was a freezing rain, and I was standing on the sideline becoming this lacrosse ice sculpture, when I said to myself, "This is it. I've got to call my mother. I've got to tell her I'm going to go to California to become a bodybuilder, because that's my dream." In my dorm room, I had pictures on the wall of all the big, muscled monsters. I knew, "This is what I want to be. I want to be a bodybuilder." You may think, "A Jew and a bodybuilder? That doesn't match. It's like milk and meat, socks and sandals. Jewish and bodybuilder don't go together."

Bodybuilding made me feel great, and I stood up straighter. People recognized me. I was training every day. I saw myself as big and strong. I'd look in that mirror, posing like I saw in the magazines, and I wasn't a skinny kid becoming muscular—I was a fat kid becoming a muscular one. When I went home to tell my parents, my dad said, "Look, you have a dream? Then you go do it."

Before I left, all of my friends, the gang of guys I used to hang with, said things like, "What are you doing, man?" I said, "I'm going to go to California; I'm going to become Mr. America." One said, "You're a fat joke. You're never going to make it to California." They all said stuff like that. "There's no way, man." "You'll never make it. You'll be home by summer." I hear those voices sometimes still today. It gets me. I love when people bet against me.

> *I love when people bet against me.*

My passion has always been bodybuilding. But I never became Mr. America. I came in second place in Mr. Southern California. The guy who beat me was on steroids. I'd made a very conscious decision that this was not a good thing. I was 19. So I wasn't Mr. America. But I said to myself, "I just can't go back. I love training. I love working out. I will do something with this. I don't know what it is, but I'm not going back to New York." So I became the first guy to do personal fitness training. It happened by accident. A girl asked me to help her at my apartment complex. She was getting ready to do a Club Med commercial, and I got her in shape. She was connected to other people in town. One person led to the second, and the third person was Steven Spielberg. He and I became like brothers. To have someone like that and Harrison Ford and Bette Midler and Priscilla Presley and Steve Royce and Warren Beatty all meant a lot. Here I was going through these people's homes. I knew this was the moment.

Still, you have to keep following through with yourself. You look at yourself in the mirror sometimes and know you have a great idea. You write it down at night, and you wake up the next morning with all the excitement and enthusiasm to pull off this idea, this dream, and all of a sudden you start thinking of the reasons why you can't. By the time you've had coffee and gotten into your car, you stop thinking about succeeding because you start toying with the notion that you can't do this.

What helped me get past that was being around the kind of people I was with every day. I learned the greatest lesson of all. I realized, wait a second, they're no different from me. The only difference is they had a dream, they never quit on their dream, and they never took no for an answer. And that said to me, "You know what? I might never direct *E.T.*, but I'm going to have my own success." That was the moment. I became famous by association. I was the first guy to do personal fitness training, make it into an occupation, and parley that into videos and books. Ted Turner gave me my start doing the "Fitness Break" on Cable News Network in 1982. Ted became a friend and a mentor.

The thing is, never quit. Because you never know when the coach is going to look down the bench and say, "Stedman, there's nobody else in here. You've been sitting here staring at me for a long enough time—get in there already." And now you're up. You've got to be ready.

Here's my legacy, what they can put on my tombstone: Take a shot. Be passionate. And don't quit. The last thing you want to have happen in your life is to look in that mirror when you're 30 or 40 or 50 or 60, and say, "You know, I had this chance. I should have taken a try at this thing. I was going to do this. But I didn't." That's what drives people crazy. The worst thing that can happen to you is that you fail. Everybody fails at something. It happens. I did. We all do. Try to learn from your failure. You also can tell the kind of person you are, and the kind of people you are around, by how you handle yourself not just when you're at the mountain, but when you're in the deepest, darkest ditch. Never quit! Never!

Take a shot. Be passionate. And don't quit.

QUESTIONS TO CONSIDER

1. Have you figured out what you love to do? If not, find out. Becoming great at something takes a lot of persistence. You've got to love what you do, or it'll just be too hard. Look at a list of your passions and choose wisely.

____

____

____

2. How will you express your core values as you pursue your chosen passion?

____

____

____

3. How will you measure your progress to know that you're getting really good at it? You need measurable incremental goals to provide constant real-time feedback. That's the thing about ballgames—you get feedback every swing.

____

____

____

CHAPTER 10

Adjustments and Tune-ups for Your Identity

It's like the Wizard of Oz. We're looking for a wizard, seeking a heart, a brain, courage, and the wizard says you already have these things. All you need to do is use them. When you believe in your great indomitable self, then all things are possible.
—Marva Collins

Rob turned on his television and was flipping through the channels when an episode of the reality show *X-Factor* caught his eye. Though he didn't usually watch such shows, one contestant kept him from flipping to the next channel. He watched 17-year-old Emmanuel Kelly tell how he and his brother had been found as severely injured infants in war-torn Iraq, with no way to know how old they were because they had no birth certificates. Kelly said of his adoptive Australian mother, "I was born in the middle of a war zone. My brother and I were found by nuns in a box in a park, in a shoebox.... It was like looking at an angel when my mum walked through the orphanage door. She brought us both to Australia for surgery originally and then, sort of, Mum fell in love with both of us. My hero would have to be my mother."

With no left hand, and holding to the microphone stand with part of a right hand, the young man sang Lennon's song *Imagine*. "Imagine there's no countries, it isn't hard to do, nothing to kill or die for...." Rob was struck by how comfortable Kelly seemed in his own skin. When Kelly rushed into the arms of his mother and brother after his performance, the love that had generated this confident identity glowed from the group hug. Growing up as he had, nurtured in such raw affection after a rocky start, made all the difference for Kelly.

Rob turned off the TV and began mulling over how some quite healthy and whole people seem filled with doom and gloom, whereas this singer had just bubbled with a healthy and whole identity. The confidence and exuberance of the young singer compared to all those with doubts who have so much more than the Iraqi orphan was a punch to the stomach for Rob—and should have been a wake-up call for more appreciation and zest in life by quite a few viewers.

The phone rang. Rob answered and heard Dutch's voice. "Could you stand a cup of coffee? Hop over to our usual spot. There's something I'd like you to hear."

Rob entered the coffee shop barely ten minutes later, and there sat Dutch with Stella "Best Deal" Sturgis. You couldn't drive anywhere in Blakenfield without seeing a colossal image of her on a billboard or on the side a truck she'd loaned out to those who bought homes through her agency. She was a regular commercial star, too, and her ever-present claim for always having "the best deal around" was her catch phrase.

Rob got a cup of coffee and was lowering himself into a chair at their table as he joined them when Dutch said, "Stella is having an identity crisis."

"Well, I wouldn't call it a crisis," she said. "I'd say an epiphany." Stella had smoked in her younger years and now had a voice like gravel being poured out of a bucket. That, coupled with the kind of stern face you might find on a school librarian at a military school, should have made her an imposing figure. But Rob had known her for years, both from seeing her at public events where she'd been a prominent community leader, and from mowing lawns for her real estate agency. She might sound like a Marine drill sergeant, but she was as sweet as anyone's favorite aunt.

Stella turned to Rob. "I recently got the listing for the storefront where Dutch used to have his book shop. Dutch told me you worked there for him, so he thought you'd enjoy hearing this. I was going through the empty store, looking around, and it started me thinking. You may not know this, because I certainly don't advertise it, but one of my secret little deals with the world is always to leave things better than I found them."

"When she sold all that acreage for that development in the south end of town, she wrangled to set aside enough land for a ball field and talked them into adding hiking and biking trails around the development," Dutch said. "A lot of people don't know that."

"I shoot for little things, too," she said. "I've helped wrangle financing from banks for young couples getting started. I always make sure there are no unpleasant surprises for homebuyers who go through me. I've had foundations firmed up and new roofs put on. But I don't say that to brag—I tell you this to illustrate something I've learned about myself."

Rob lowered his cup and leaned closer. "Do tell." It seemed everyone had more dimensions since he'd been paying attention to identity, and that made them more interesting.

"The thing is," Stella said, "I used to thrill in the chase, in besting competing agencies and closing a deal while they were still getting into gear. I was a Vince Lombardi kind of gal. For me, winning wasn't everything—it was the only thing. I used to need to be that bigger-than-life character radiating in-your-face success. I was winning, all right, but I didn't always enjoy those glances in the mirror. Maybe trying to always do something extra good for my clients was compensation. At any rate, I sat down with myself and said it was decision time. I've had a long and successful career, although I might have been a bit misguided about what 'success' was really all about, and I'm old enough to retire. I also asked myself what I really liked about what I did. My answer was, I really got the most kick out of making my clients' lives a

I really got the most kick out of making my clients' lives a little better, by going the extra mile for them.

little better, by going the extra mile for them. And I finally figured out that the little things in life wear people down or lift them up. So I asked myself, why don't I try to provide a little lift here and there on a full-time basis?"

Rob's coffee had cooled enough for him to take a sip. He did so and waited.

Stella rubbed her hands together, and a glimmer showed in her eyes. "Here's my plan. I'm going to leave my business to my two nieces, and I'm going to open a thrift shop in the storefront where Dutch used to have his bookstore. This town doesn't have one, so it meets a need. Plus, I'll be retired and in better shape than most, so I don't even need a salary. Everything I clear can go to charities. If I get too much stock, I can get folks to haul some of it to the nearest Goodwill. And not only will the store do some good, but it can be a community spot again, with bake sales out front and clubs meeting there, just like when Dutch had his store. What do you think?"

Rob glanced toward Dutch, who was beaming. Rob said, "I think it's a great idea. But what made you decide to take this particular leap?"

"Ah, good question, my young man. Sometimes people, well-intentioned or otherwise, get off track, particularly about what really matters. They may even need to reinvent themselves. Sometimes they can fix things themselves; other times, they need the help of friends and family. When I realized what really makes me happy, I redefined success for myself and decided to do something about it," Stella said. "I want to like the person I see in the mirror a little more each day, and I plan to do that by spending each day helping people make their lives a little better. I think a community thrift shop will be a perfect place to do just that."

A couple months later, Rob drove by and saw Girl Scouts selling cookies outside the old store. He found a parking place and went over to the store where he'd once sold quite a few books. Inside, Stella looked up from unpacking a box and waved to him. The shelves were filled and clothes hung from racks. "Who'd ever have thought that a person could end up with so much from other people's used stuff?" she said. The town had sure rallied around the shop (with a little of Dutch's influence) and the goods had come pouring in, from churches, clubs, individuals, and just about everywhere. Stella looked around at all the merchandise, as if a little amazed herself at how her little miracle was coming along. She pointed toward an oak dresser with a beveled-glass mirror. "Now I can look in there and feel pretty good about what I see."

She took a hard, clear look at her identity and redefined what success meant.

Stella did something not everyone does. She took a hard, clear look at her identity and redefined what success meant. To her, the refreshing feel of honest, helpful toil was freedom.

STEP # 8—WIN BY A DECISION

What you are in this world is the result of the decisions you have made so far in your life. The choices you make now will be one of your greatest challenges. Consider carefully how they will have an impact on your personal life, family, profession and career, and, of course, your long-term vision.

DISCUSSION

The successful person makes a habit of doing what the failing person doesn't like to do.
—Thomas Edison

If you've been on the Internet, you're no stranger to people who add comments to news stories. They may use aliases that seem to free them to say some nasty things. That's what identity is not. That's a masked mob feeding the mean wolf inside. If those same people were constrained to be transparent, to use a real name, like Ralph B. Jackson instead of ScooterPie7, would they say some of the same things? I doubt it. Yet some people aren't kind and value-driven when hiding behind the mask of a fake name. Some are mean. Is that where you want to be? Hopefully you can be you—and openly you!

Aside from the transparency issue, life can dish up a lot of curves in the path to your identity. You may stumble and face obstacles, even personal disasters. You need to be prepared to pick yourself up, dust yourself off, and start all over again. You might even look up, as Stella did, and not like everything you see about yourself. Sometimes you can be your own worst enemy. You need to learn how to avoid that—or, at least, how to recover if you find yourself headed in that direction.

We keep bumping up against seemingly different concepts of identity. As you read the story of Syd Field, you might see it the way Syd tells it—that he progressed through a sequence of extreme identity makeovers. Or you might conclude that the emergence of his true identity just took a little while. See what you think.

Profile in Success
Syd Field

Syd Field is acclaimed as the "guru of all screenwriters" by CNN and "the most sought-after screenwriting teacher in the world" by the Hollywood Reporter. *The internationally celebrated author of eight books on screenwriting, his book* Screenplay *is considered "the Bible" of the film industry, published in some 28 languages and used in more than 450 major colleges and universities around the country. He has conducted screenwriting workshops all over the world and has been a special script consultant to the governments of Argentina, Australia, Austria, Brazil, Germany, Israel, Mexico, and more. He has been commissioned to conduct special executive workshops by the Disney Studios, 20th Century Fox, Universal Studios, the Nike Corporation, and others. Field was inducted into the prestigious Final Draft Hall of Fame in 2006 and is currently on faculty in the celebrated Masters of Professional Writing Program at USC. Much of Hollywood uses his screenplay paradigm, or rebels against it, so Syd has made his mark. Still, he has learned that even though he has a firm handle on his own identity, he has to stay light on his feet and be able to reinvent himself. Here is his story, in his own words.*

When I was growing up, I had to cope with having an older brother—four years older, to be exact—who was the apple of my parents' eye. They named my father's furniture company, Morton's Furniture, after him. He was always such a "good" boy that he never did anything wrong in their eyes and was held up to me as a shining example of how I was supposed to be. I rebelled and decided that if he was the "good one," I was going to get even by being the "bad one" and getting in trouble a lot of the time.

This was just my stubbornness at work. So growing up, I, along with all my friends, were more into rebellion than anything else. In high school, we were the guys endlessly in some kind of trouble. We were also the star athletes on the track team, so we got away with it most of the time. My family still remembers what a concern I became to my mother after my father died when I was 12. She feared that I wasn't going to make it in life because I was always getting into trouble and I showed no apparent aptitude for anything other than athletics. By the time we graduated high school, Jimmy Dean was a rising star. My friend Frank met Dean by accident, and Jimmy started hanging out with us as we strolled down Hollywood Boulevard looking for trouble—and find it we would. We got in a lot of fights and ended up in juvenile hall. We were everything being a rebel was about.

Jimmy Dean somehow found in us a freedom and another way to look at his life. Instead of living the structured life of an actor, for him it became the unstructured life of freedom, of which acting was a part. About a year after Jimmy made *Rebel Without a Cause*, we realized that our group of guys were the "bad guys" model for the movie. So we started to play that role full on. And then my mother died. My aunt accused me of murdering my mother. She didn't really mean it. She was sick with loss and grief. Of course, it took years for me to understand that she didn't mean it. But when my mother died on my birthday, I started to turn my personality around. Out of choice, I didn't continue as the overt, getting-in-trouble, loud-mouthed attention getter. I became the quiet and introverted one. I said, "I'm not going to be an athlete. I'm not going to run track anymore." (I was a member of the track team at USC the year we became national champions.)

Instead, I went to U.C. Berkeley and morphed from being a loudmouth attention getter to a quiet, introverted person who focused on being "good." I attempted to fulfill the promise I had made my mother just before she died, that I was at heart a good boy. This meant I would become a professional person: doctor, lawyer, Indian chief—whatever she wanted, that's what I was going to be.

At Berkeley, I was drifting, not knowing where I was going and still searching for what I wanted. I started acting and had good success. Then I met my mentor, Jean Renoir, the French film director, screenwriter, actor, producer, and author. As a film director and actor, he made more than 40 films, from the silent era through the end of the 1960s. As an author, he wrote the definitive biography of his father, the painter Pierre-Auguste Renoir, and as a man, he changed the direction of my life. Renoir said to me, "The future is film—don't waste your time with English literature, don't waste your time trying to be a professional person, the future is film!" He wrote me a letter saying to the UCLA film department, "Let this kid in."

And so they did. I went to UCLA for a year. I was there with Ray Manzarek and Jim Morrison. They were punk rockers at the time, and they created a garage band called the Doors. We all made films together and hung out together, and then they went into music, and my uncle got me a job as a gofer in the film business. I worked in shipping at Wolper, a studio praised for *Roots*, *Willy Wonka*, and *Thorn Birds*. First and foremost, Wolper was a documentary film producer. This was really the period that defined my life, because it gave me a direction. In retrospect, that's when I found out I had choices to make in my life. Film was a big arena. If I wanted to be in film, what did I want to do in film? And the answer was, well, go into production in some way. But serendipitous circumstances drove me to look for a writer's job. Because I was the only one at Wolper who really figured out how the library worked, I volunteered to do research.

When I was at Wolper doing research for five years, I was still a young kid, and I learned that I could find stuff. That was my gift—I could find stuff. I found the actual Bay of Pigs footage that was shot on the boat as they were going to invade Cuba. I found Grace Kelly's first modeling spread, shot when she was 17 years old in high school. I found the first film Marilyn Monroe ever made—a Union 76 commercial. She went by her maiden name of Norma Jean Baker at that time.

I was learning that I could find things if I set my mind to it. I became aware that, with this change in mental strategy and energy, I could put that energy out into the world and opportunities would start to find me. I could then make different choices about who I wanted to be as a person and what I wanted to do. I remember the "aha!" moment when I recognized that I could make the choice to be a success or a nonsuccess. That literally changed my life. In that moment, I realized that I could choose the life I wanted.

With this change in mental strategy and energy, I could put that energy out into the world and opportunities would start to find me.

This was also when I had the opportunity to write my first book and to start teaching. This was back in the '70s. These were times of great exploration and great experimentation. I was fortunate to be within the crucible of that change in the film industry. We were all setting out along this unknown path of experimentation in making television the way we wanted to see television. You can't do that now, of course—but that's how we started, going around to show what could be done and creating what we called entertainment documentaries, the forerunner of shows like *Law and Order*.

When I started out teaching, I was terrible. I was the worst you can imagine, because I had this position that, if I'm hired to be the teacher and you guys are the students, I have to know something that you don't. It made me just the worst teacher. Students were leaving in droves every night. I could figure out it wasn't working; so, I thought, “Why don't I be a student and they be the teacher?” opened up class to answer questions from the students. I answered from my own experience as a reader, a writer, and now a teacher. I began to realize that everybody has the same questions regarding how to write a screenplay.

How do you tell your story? How do you structure a story? How do you create the characters, write more effective dialogue, and shape strong and complex characters? This became the structure for the book. I read a lot of screenplays along the way—at least 10,000 to 15,000, and probably 20,000 by now. I've sold screenplays, had a few produced, and had quite a few optioned. As I'm looking back, I see that there were certain signposts that directed me as I was moving along this path. I didn't even know that teaching was one of them until I found out that I could take questions from people and not be an ass in front of the class or assume I knew something they didn't know. I went back to writing and finally sat down to pull chapter outlines together for a book. I wrote an introduction and then two chapters, and got it sold within two weeks. I've been writing and teaching all over the world ever since.

Now the whole business of film is being reinvented. The power of the big studios and the mainstream media is vanishing, just like the world changed in the music industry. All of us in the business have to reinvent our identities and roles in the business of film and television.

What's interesting to me is the growth I'm going through right now. At this moment in time, and after all these years,

I'm still not clear about understanding who I am in terms of identity, because I'm changing now with the current of the times, reinventing my identity as I am carried along by the current. Identity to me is a conscious thing, and any conscious thing lives and grows and changes and adapts to the times. If you don't adapt, it's over. You see that all the time. People who can't adapt get locked in nonsuccess until they perish.

People who cannot adapt to the present time is what Sam Peckinpah, one of my mentors, used to write about. He believed that there were unchanged men in changing times, so he made *The Wild Bunch*, in which you have four outlaws who are out of time. In a similar vein, you have *Butch Cassidy and the Sundance Kid*. The characters go to Bolivia because they can't adapt to the times of the railroad, to the telephone, to the check; they're out of business because all they know how to do is rob banks. In *The Wild Bunch*, it's the same way—all they know how to do is rob banks. Their trade, their identity, is of a bank robber. However, at that time, in 1907, things had changed, and they didn't know how to adapt to the change. So this idea about unchanged men in changing times is really important, and that's exactly what I'm beginning to understand.

People who can't adapt get locked in nonsuccess until they perish.

I either have to adapt or it's over. Period.

QUESTIONS TO CONSIDER

1. Do you tend to be your own worst enemy? List a few of your favorite ways.

   ____

   ____

   ____

2. Are things you rebel against controlling you?

   ____

   ____

   ____

3. Syd Field talked about some of the important mentors in his life. Who could you ask to become your mentor?

   ____

   ____

   ____

CHAPTER 11

Bringing It All Together—Committing to Your Vision

Where there is no vision,
the people perish.
—Proverbs 29:18

Rob made his way down the long empty hallway, listening to the noise of his sneakers squeaking on the polished flooring. Not sneaking, he thought, as he stopped in front of the door he wanted and knocked.

"Come in."

Professor Draper turned from his credenza holding a bone-white cup and saucer. The tag of a tea bag hung from one side of the cup. He wore a tweed jacket, but at least one without leather elbow patches.

"Do you want a cup?"

Rob shook his head.

His advisor nodded toward one of the two guest chairs near his desk. He eased himself down into his chair.

"You're back a touch early. Was it an eventful summer back in Blakenfield, or were you run out of town?"

"Eventful. I see now why you suggested spending my time there might be productive. I also see why you suggested those two business courses I took earlier, along with all the units in Computer Engineering."

"I'm your advisor, but also a touch unorthodox. I believe a lot happens outside the classroom that is also part of learning. Most people need to explore their important life insights on their own—with the right guidance, of course." Professor Draper's eye twinkled the way it did when he was enthused. "I'm anxious to hear all, and especially how the business courses helped."

"Well, they helped in a way I hadn't expected. I ended up thinking a lot about identity this summer, mine as well as the identities of others. I found it a deeper subject than I expected, and also that I didn't know nearly as much as I thought I did."

"It is ever thus when learning the really good stuff."

"One of the really odd insights, and I attribute this to the business courses, was that I got to thinking about identity the way you'd think about a brand. On the way home I read *Do You Matter?—How Great Design Will Make People Love Your Company,* from the suggested reading list you gave us. The authors say that a useful way to look at brand is that it is like an individual's character or identity. 'What matters is what people think and feel about your brand. And you don't control that. While you cannot control what people feel, what you must do is provide influence and make sure that how you're doing this authentically represents who you are and what you offer.' The real zinger for me was the line, 'Your brand lives in your customer's gut—it's not what you say it is, it's what they say it is.' Successful companies pride themselves on having core values and want those reflected in their products. They seek out customers who share those values and are committed to offering them great experiences and making their lives a little better—sometimes a lot better. The amazing thing, at least to me, is that each of us can follow that same path—have a vision, the way companies have a mission statement, keep our actions in line with our values—and that should almost always lead to success."

Your brand lives in your customer's gut—it's not what you say it is, it's what they say it is.

"Hmm...I believe you really have had a productive summer."

"That's not all. One of the things we can learn from companies is that they are in danger when their products become commodities. When they don't generate goods and services based on emotional consumer needs, then they have a fragile bond. They start not to matter anymore. Take Starbucks. If it's only about price and product, they can get hammered when McDonald's starts competing with cappuccinos.

Companies that matter do so because they have formed a genuine emotional bond with consumers and are dedicated to the quality of their customer's experience. I'm not saying people should think of themselves as selling a product. But I do think you should take a look at your life in that light—your values and the experience people have when they are with you. So I arrived home with the question in mind: 'How can I make people's lives a little better?'"

"Sounds like you had a pretty insightful time of it. Now, tell me about the people. I always like to hear about people."

STEP #9—COMMIT TO YOUR VISION

Put all your energy and effort toward achieving your goals. Enthusiasm and commitment generate excellence, and that leads to success. The challenge is to develop the ability to coexist with the world as it changes, never giving in and never giving up.

Profile in Success
Eleanor Josaitis

The irony of commitment is that it's deeply liberating—
in work, in play, in love.
—Anne Morriss

The 1967 riots left metropolitan Detroit, like many urban American cities, sharply divided along racial lines. Watching the violence on TV in the comfort of her suburban home, a young white homemaker became so outraged, she abandoned her middle-class white neighborhood and moved with her husband and her five kids to the demographically black downtown shortly after the riots ended. Her sudden change of lifestyle was unwelcome in her family. Eleanor Josaitis was disowned by her father-in-law and was asked to change her name by her brother-in-law. When word got out that she was bent on bringing blacks and whites together, she endured hate mail and firebombs.

"There were moments when we were terrified," she sighed. "But that didn't change what we had to do." Josaitis recruited the people who showed up as volunteers for Focus: HOPE, which today provides food to 43,000 seniors, mothers, and children each month; career training programs in machining, engineering, and information technologies; child care; business conference facilities; community arts projects; and other outreach initiatives. Focus: HOPE has 500 team members and 51,000 supporters. That's what is possible when you align a whole community—young, old, black, and white.

"Anything worth doing can't be done alone," Josaitis said. "There's been too much hero worship about how just one person does it all. At one point, we craved charismatic leaders, but that has been pretty well discredited, as we've seen smooth operators go to jail or fall way short of overhyped expectations. Well, you can make a difference in a business or your community, but not if it's just about you. It's about finding other people who get inspired by their own belief that they can make a difference in a similar way—you've got to find other leaders who can make it happen with you!"

You can make a difference in a business or your community, but not if it's just about you. It's about finding other people who get inspired by their own belief that they can make a difference in a similar way.

"It is all about alignment between what you are and what you do—about making that fit together," Josaitis said, pounding her fist into her hand. There's always a little righteousness seeping from every one of her sentences. "You've got to recruit yourself to something you believe in, and then you have to recruit yourself to the right job—then go out there and seize the opportunity. And if you need a leader, you've got to recruit that person, too. It's about lining yourself up with a role where you feel as connected with the other people as you feel with the cause. When you feel that way, you've got a team."

Recruiting people to her team, she said, is about discovering "people whose dreams are like yours—and then not letting a single one of those folks get out of your sight or off the hook without doing something about it!"

Enduringly successful people are people who, at some point in their life, got over the syndrome of thinking, "We're all in this alone!"

Senator John McCain learned this lesson the hard way.

Profile in Success

Senator John McCain

"Well, when I was a young pilot, I believed that all glory was self-glory. I believed that I needed no one—that I was perfectly capable of doing whatever I needed to do by myself. And I learned as a prisoner of war in Hanoi that I was reliant and dependent on others, both for my physical well-being and then for my mental well-being. When I failed, they would pick me up and encourage me, and help me to go back into the fray again."

"The great privilege of my life was to serve in the company of heroes, a place where I observed a thousand acts of courage, compassion, and love."

Amazingly, McCain, who survived five and a half years as a prisoner of war, described his brutal experience as transforming. He said he was grateful to Vietnam for strengthening his self-confidence and teaching him that he could trust his own judgment and that he didn't have to give up his sense of self to feel connected to other people.

"There is no greater feeling in life—no greater freedom—than to know you can be yourself and part of a group that is engaged in a cause that is greater than you are."

"There is no greater feeling in life—no greater freedom—than to know you can be yourself and part of a group that is engaged in a cause that is greater than you are," said McCain.

I like this quote from Senator McCain because it speaks to the heart of knowing who you are—being clear about your identity, your values, and what matters to you—along with making a commitment to a vision of creating value in the world. This is your passport to success.

Now it's up to you. I thought it would be helpful for you to have the Nine-Step Success Process all in one place to guide you in your work. You do have to do the work. You don't have to do it alone. Follow the process, and a great life of lasting success will be yours.

NINE-STEP SUCCESS PROCESS

Step 1: Check Your ID

Before you decide what you want for your life, you first must understand who you are, what the influences are on your life, and why you think and act the way you do. Self-awareness is where success begins. It is difficult to understand the world and how you respond to it until you first know yourself. What are your strengths? What moves you forward? What are your weaknesses? What holds you back? What are your patterns of behavior? What are your passions? Sometimes the biggest obstacles to success are those that we unconsciously put in our own paths. Past hurts, business or career downfalls, and negative attitudes hold you back. Learn from the bad experiences and failures, and let them go. Focus your life on what you love and care about, and you will never work a day in your life.

Step 2: Create Your Vision

Your vision is your life's destination. It helps you realize and explore your dreams and aspirations. It keeps you focused and helps minimize distractions. It can determine your greatness.

A well-defined vision enables you to set meaningful goals for your business or personal life. How do you envision your future and what is possible for you? Describe the short- and long-term goals that you have for your life personally and professionally.

Step 3: Develop Your Travel Plan

Prepare for the future. If you are to fulfill your vision for a better life, you must create a plan of action. When you begin to work toward your goals through a plan of action, you assert power over your life. You know who you are, where you're going, and how you're going to get there. Planning saves time, keeps you focused, and builds confidence.

Someone said that the purpose of goals is to focus our attention. The mind will not reach toward achievement until it has clear objectives. The magic begins when we set goals. It is then that the switch is turned on, the current begins to flow, and the power to accomplish becomes a reality. Whatever you focus on expands.

Step 4: Master the Rules of the Road

You need guidelines to keep you on track in pursuit of a better life. The rules are constant and enduring; they do not change. Characteristics to guide your life:

- Honesty
- Trust
- Hard work
- Determination
- Positive attitude

Step 5: Step into the Outer Limits

To grow, you have to leave your comfort zone, confront fears, and take risks. Fear of the unknown is one of the greatest obstacles you will face when you're traveling the journey of the Success Process. To be successful, you must learn to overcome that natural fear and step outside what has become comfortable and familiar. Key points to remember:

- Risk is a natural part of life.
- Staying the same is standing still.
- Change (growth) means risk.

Step 6: Pilot the Seasons of Change

If you keep doing what you have always done, you will get the same results. Learn how to create change and manage your response. Dealing with changing circumstances is important, but creating and managing your response to change in your life is probably an even greater part of the Success Process. Challenges happen when the pace of change exceeds our ability to change, and events move faster than our understanding. But with change comes opportunity and growth.

Step 7: Build Your Dream Team

No one makes it alone. Build supportive relationships, perhaps with mentors who will help you work toward your goals. Learn to trust and be trustworthy. You'll need the help and encouragement of others. With a great team helping you, you can do more than you ever could alone. Include people who care about you and believe in your goals. Trust is critical to building a strong support team. Credibility comes with a pattern of behavior. Trust is not easily earned; real trust is established over time.

Remember: Mentors pick you; you do not pick them.

Step 8: Win by a Decision

What you are in this world is largely the result of the decisions you have made so far in your life. The choices that you make will be one of your greatest challenges. How can you tell the difference between a good and a bad decision? Good decisions have desirable consequences: They help you grow and reach your goal. Bad decisions have undesirable consequences. Continue to maximize your decision-making ability by considering the impact it will have in these areas:

- Personal impact
- Family impact
- Profession and career impact
- Job impact
- Long-term vision

Step 9: Commit to Your Vision

Devote your time and energy on a consistent basis to pursue your goals and vision.

Enthusiasm and commitment generate excellence, and that leads to success. A commitment is something you live and something you renew and fulfill every day. It is doing rather than saying.

Your success is based on your commitment to discovery:

1. Discover who you are.
2. Discover how to apply this knowledge to the world you live in.
3. Make the discovery process part of your daily routine to sustain success over a lifetime.

The challenge is the ability to coexist and grow with the world as it changes, never giving in and never giving up.

Summary

During these very difficult times in our world economy, I hope you understand that you have the potential to create your life and be whomever you decide to be. You must realize that your potential as a human being is based not on how the world defines you, but on how you define yourself. Through education, hard work, and purpose, you can start to develop, evolve, and create the opportunities that define and determine your identity and your future.

When you take ownership of this, you celebrate your life every day, along with the rights and freedom to which all humans are entitled.

Enjoy the journey.

Afterword
By Stephen R. Covey

I have tremendous admiration for Stedman Graham and for the mission he has chosen. He personifies the message he has presented in this book and is a powerful example of someone who has actually defined his identity and created an enduringly successful life that is a gift to the world. I also know how genuine, deeply genuine, Stedman is about helping people discover who they are and achieve their highest potential for success.

Stedman Graham cares about the individual. He understands how someone's vision can have greater impact than their baggage, for Stedman has not allowed the challenges of his past circumstances to dictate his future. This book's important message is to live out of your imagination and not your history—to hold a vision of the possibility of a better life for you and the people you care about—and to exercise the faith and power you have within you to create that better life. Stedman is an important spokesperson for this message because, in addition to the traditional credentials of advanced educational degrees and significant national leadership positions, he brings the "street" credibility of having faced and conquered the challenges of which he speaks firsthand. Men and women, boys and girls, of all cultures and circumstances throughout the world can take heart in his example. He is a rare mentor who walks his talk.

Stedman, like many, was born into a host of troubling circumstances and emotional hardships that could have easily left him a bitter and resentful victim. How many of us would be able to sing a similar tune when uncontrollable conditions threaten to kill our hopes and dreams? It becomes easy to excuse our failures and get into a blaming mode, using our past as a hitching post, and condemning most everything around us. We may seek out friends, or even "experts," who would agree and give us more ammunition to justify our plight as we proceed to attribute every mistake and misfortune in our lives to poor environment, disturbed upbringing, or genetics. We then sink deeper and deeper into the quicksand of self-pity and victimization. Some of us might have had a father who deserted us when we were young, or an uncle who viciously abused us. Perhaps we continually had to scratch and scrape together whatever we could to survive in the face of grinding poverty. Each one of us has a story to tell—a story that is very real. In fact, such injustices and dehumanizing experiences do take their toll, sometimes a *tremendous* toll, in our lives. Yet, the difference between being influenced by and determined by is 180 degrees. The point becomes whether or not you will allow yourself to remain victimized for the rest of your life. As Stedman so eloquently teaches, "It matters not how other people define you, it matters how you define yourself."

By doing the work that only you can do for you, learning who you really are and following Stedman's "Nine-Step Success Process" for a better life, you will learn how to create a vision for your future that will, in return, produce the needed antidote for conquering the difficulties of life.

The best way to predict your future is to create it. As you apply the powerful principles Stedman has shared in this insightful book, you will create the future of your dreams. May we each follow Stedman's lead and define our identity, and in so doing create a personal passport to success.

Stephen R. Covey
Author of The 7 Habits of Highly Effective People